REMEMBER
GOD

ANNIE F. DOWNS

PUBLISHING GROUP

NASHVILLE, TENNESSEE

978-1-4336-4689-8

Published by B&H Publishing Group
Nashville, Tennessee

Dewey Classification: 231
Subject Heading: GOD \ LOVE \ CHRISTIAN LIFE

Cover design by Matt Lehman.
Author photo © Micah Kandros.

2 3 4 5 6 7 8 • 22 21 20 19 18

This one, dearest, is for you.

Foreword

When we loaded up a U-Haul and drove to Nashville to start a new season of life in a new town for our family of six, we only knew three people in the entire city. Annie Downs was one of them. My wife, Rea, and I have known Annie for twenty years. We were all part of a college ministry together at the University of Georgia. (Go Dawgs!) It was one of those movements that marks your life forever and leaves you saying, "I'll go anywhere and do anything for You, God." God took us up on that prayer twenty years later when He called us to Cross Point Church. God had taken Annie up on her prayer, moving her here ten years before. Being new to Nashville and knowing Annie . . . it's not fair. If you know Annie, you know the whole city. Annie Downs is friends with everyone.

But most important, Annie is a friend of God. You hear it when she prays. It's in her eyes when she talks about Jesus. We see it at the dinner table in how she loves our kids, and it's evident in the way she loves our church. I've figured it out: the reason Annie has so many friends in Nashville is because the closer you get to Annie, the closer you feel to God. When you get around Annie, you can sense the presence of her favorite friend.

You'll sense God's presence in this book because, in these pages, Annie is going to let you close. Probably closer than in anything she's ever written. Possibly closer than anything you've ever read. This is high-risk as an author. Man, it's high-risk as a human. When you let people that close into questions and convictions, wrestling and wandering, uncertainty and surrender, it's high-risk, but it's also high-reward. The reward of this book is that it's going to help you with your memory problems.

As humans we have two kinds of memory problems: we forget the things we're supposed to remember, and we remember the things we should forget, kind of like spiritual amnesia. When that happens, you don't need a cliché; you need a friend. A friend to come alongside you and remind you of the truth that matters most. The kind of truth that is still going to be true one hundred years from now. This book contains that kind of truth, and Annie Downs is that kind of friend. As you read *Remember God*, you'll feel all the feels. That's just your heart waking up to the glorious reality of what happens when you remember God well. But the peace that you will feel when you finish the book, I believe this peace comes from the greater reality that, in Christ, God remembers you.

I pray a hundred-year anointing over this book, and my prayer for you is that these words grow your faith and impact your life in such a way that matters one hundred years from now.

Kevin Queen, Lead Pastor
Cross Point Church, Nashville, Tennessee

O God, Your incarnate Son Jesus Christ is the eternal Word in whom may be read the good news at the heart of all that You are doing. Grant to all who speak or write what many may hear or read, that love of truth which leads to love of God, and that love of God which makes communication of thought a good and holy thing, through Jesus Christ our Lord. Amen.

Canon Ian Jagger,
Archdeacon of Durham Cathedral
Durham, England

Introduction

What say we all just take a deep breath.

I need one.

I bet you do too.

When you pick up a new book, there's a reason. You're looking for something. You may not know what exactly, but something. And with all my heart, I hope you find it.

When I start typing, I'm looking for something.

And with all my heart, I hope I find it too.

———

I've kind of gotten into yoga lately. This new studio opened in my neighborhood, and lots of my friends began to practice there. They play loud music, mostly pop and hip-hop, and I'm almost guaranteed to have a friend in any class I take. That's pretty much all the push I need to exercise—great music and my pals.

As I started to attend classes, I really began to love it, but . . . I need a lot of guidance. So rather than being the annoying gal in the back row who needs a personal tutor, I chose instead to watch some YouTube videos with instructions and bought a mat (also with instructions, like showing me exactly where to put my hands and feet).

I try to mostly sign up for Emmy's classes, because we're friends, and if someone is going to make me do a standing split (Google it, and then die a little at how hard it is), I want to at least believe she likes me as a person. I also frequent the Wednesday night class taught by Koula, but it is VERY HARD and sometimes makes me feel like crying. Whatever.

The start of each class is the same. Child's pose, which is like you're bowing to someone, arms stretched fully in front of you, shins on the mat, body folded over your bent legs. Then Emmy tells us to breathe in through our nose and sigh out through our mouth. It feels silly the first time, making a loud sighing sound, but now it feels natural. It truly is like pushing out whatever has been aching inside of me that day, then sighing about the things I tried to hold in during a busy morning or a stressful meeting or a hard FaceTime conversation.

It's cleansing, it really is. The breathing and sighing prepares me for the work ahead that my body is going to do. Yoga hurts as we go, it stretches me, but it's always worth it, even if I end class collapsed down again into child's pose. Covered in sweat. Muscles aching.

Breathing. Sighing.

———

I'm breathing now. Sitting here, writing, wondering how this thing is going to turn out. For the first time in my writing life, I don't see the end of this book yet, because I don't know the end of the story. And it is so scary to me. You've probably heard me say before how, when I write books, I don't feel like my job is to create them out of thin air but to "find" them. The books I'm meant to write are already sitting on a heavenly shelf, and my job is to find each one, almost like mining for treasure as God directs me, whispers to me, and brings themes and stories to my mind. (I also like to think my grandmothers, since they missed seeing my books published on earth, have dedicated a portion of their bookshelves in heaven to my works—the ones already in print and the ones that none of us know yet.)

But this one? This book is different.

I'm writing it, but I'm reading it too. I'm listening and learning and figuring out with each stroke of the key that I need this. I need to remember God.

———

Andrew asked me to come over to record a podcast one day—a Thursday. His wife, Alison, one of my best friends, was there with us, sitting on the couch drinking coffee. Their three daughters, Ella, Sadie, and Charlotte, were all at Vacation Bible School . . . much to my sadness because I find them endlessly entertaining.

Andrew and I sat down at the dining room table, each to our own microphone. He started with some basic questions about my job and how I got here professionally. Then we started talking about this book, the writing I was soon to be doing here.

And we talked about who I was writing it for.

With each of my books, I know exactly who I hope is on the other side of these words. In fact, I do more than just picture them in my mind. I frame a picture on my desk of the exact person or people I'm thinking about when I'm sitting there, typing my brains out.

Except I hadn't done it yet this time. The person, or people, weren't clear to me. I'd thought about it a few times but hadn't landed on the photograph I wanted to frame on my desk. But as soon as Andrew asked me, about *this* book, I suddenly knew exactly who I've been writing for all along.

"This one is different than anything I've ever written," I said, as tears loosened and began streaming down my cheeks, "because this one, I think I'm writing . . . for me."

And that makes me cry.

Because if I don't come out of this thing ruthlessly believing, then you may not either. So I'm trying—gosh, I'm trying so hard—to grab on and not let go, to believe with all my guts even when my life is just not turning out like I thought it would. I thought I would be somewhere totally different as I start into this book. And yet, here I am. Here *you* are. And here we go.

———

What I do know so far of this story has been as shocking and beautiful as anything I've ever lived. But I think I'm as surprised about the next pages as you are. Which, side note for those of you hoping to be authors: THIS IS THE WRONG WAY TO WRITE A BOOK. It isn't safe. It isn't fun. It is borderline terrifying and possibly unwise. (My agent and editor will let me know soon enough.) It's like I'm driving a train down a set of tracks that God is building right in my line of sight, barely in front of the fast-moving train—engine, caboose, dining car, and all. Not the most comforting view because . . . *Hi!* Trains need lots of tracks. And I feel like I don't have them.

But even with this fear, I'm breathing. I'm breathing in what I know to be true, and I'm sighing out the parts I can't reconcile between what my heart knows and what my eyes see. Because they just aren't always the same, are they?

I'm afraid this story is going to break my heart. And you're going to see it. And I'll be too far in it to get any of us out. I'm afraid I'm going to spend the next chapters telling you of His provision and kindness, and then we'll get to the end and it won't look the way we thought it would, and it will hurt. I'm afraid it's going to shift and turn and the tracks are going to fall off a cliff or just disappear—and it's not that I will be mad at God for building them wrong; I'll be mad at me for getting on the train and convincing you to ride along with me.

But as much as I wish this were an easier story to tell, I also think this is where we are meant to go. We are just so much better suited living a life where He is in control and we are not. Christians love to talk about how "God is in control." It's a kitschy thing to say. But it's a much different thing when you see the train tracks of your life are absolutely not going where you thought they would and you can't do anything about it. So it's beautiful. And terrible. And I'm scared.

But I hear Him in the back of my mind, reminding me that we finish every story we start together, He and I. It's actually one of the things God is really known for: Finishing. Completing. Not leaving things undone. And that will be true here as well. This story of His kindness, the one I'm about to tell you, WILL have an ending. And by the time we get there, God will have done it all, and I will know it and you will know it. And we will never forget Him.

Remember that.

Remember God.

I'm at a new coffee shop today in Nashville, one I haven't visited before. It's Monday after a busy work weekend and I'm just exhausted. My brain wants to rest; my calendar says to write. I'm not only struggling to find the words, I'm struggling to find the pictures in my mind that I want to describe for you. So I've pulled out photographs today, to see with my eyes what I can't conjure up in my mind.

To see Notre Dame.

I was fourteen years old the first time I saw the Notre Dame Cathedral in Paris. I remember the exterior as being lighter in color than I thought, this edifice of barely gray stone that traveled up into the sky higher than I imagined.

Seeing it was different than standing at the base of a skyscraper in New York City, because I knew the cathedral was built by hand. The height of the spires, the flying buttresses, the detailed statues, the gargoyles, all built and hand-carved hundreds of years ago. They first broke ground on it in 1163 and Notre Dame was completed in 1365. Yes, it took two hundred years to build that building. That's unfathomable to me. I can't envision anyone in our day starting any project knowing it likely wouldn't be completed until five generations into the future.

I have pictures of my high school best friends and I, sitting outside the cathedral, waiting on a bench. I'm wearing a pink sweater and purple hiking boots, which should just tell you everything you ever wanted to know about my teenage self. I also have a picture printed out and labeled in a scrapbook of the moment I walked inside.

The north rose stained glass window was like nothing I had ever seen. There it was, straight ahead, what seemed like miles away—the blues and pinks and yellows—a bright spot in a darker massive room. I couldn't stop staring at the light shining through it or marveling that someone had created every piece, stained it, sealed it in place, and then (and I seriously do not know how someone using thirteenth-century equipment could do this) raised it and positioned it so many stories up.

You can't get close enough to see this feature with your bare eyes, but the center of the north rose is Jesus as a baby and His mother, Mary. It's an incredible piece of art. The whole window is. The whole room is. The whole building is.

(To be fair, all of Paris is, isn't it?)

I've been back to Notre Dame a few times since. And every time I'm there, I can't help but think about the centuries of people who have sat in those pews before me. I think of all the people who have gathered there for one reason.

Because they believed in God. And wanted to remember Him.

———

My assistant, Eliza, and I travel together quite a bit, about three weekends a month for roughly eight months of the year. We rarely get tired of each other (separate hotel rooms is clutch), and we never run out of life stories or God stories to tell.

A few years ago, we realized that every city where we went for me to speak at a conference, church, or event began to look the same—just the inside of a plane, the inside of a hotel, the inside of a church or event space. It felt like we were wasting these opportunities a bit. We thought, hey—we're in ARGYLE, TEXAS, for heaven's sake. We should see it! We're in BOSTON. We're in INDIANA, PENNSYLVANIA. We're in LEWISTON, IDAHO. But we weren't seeing cities; we weren't experiencing culture; we weren't eating local. We were missing the best parts of the travel side of our jobs.

So we created a little something called Tour de Tastebuds. (Probably better known to some of you as #tourdetastebuds.) It started out simple. In every city where we traveled, Eliza and I would try to find the most hole-in-the-wall, local, delicious restaurant. We didn't want a chain; we didn't want fancy. We wanted the place we would pick on a Tuesday night with our family or friends if we lived in this particular city. And after eating, we would ask ourselves: Is this place in middle Alabama better than the meal we had last week in middle California? Up-or-down vote. On to the next place.

Then one fateful day, a few months into the competition, standing outside a barbecue restaurant in Fort Wayne, Indiana, we disagreed. I said the meal was the number-two restaurant experience of our fall season; she said it was number-one. I was floored and we were out of sync.

So we created a scoring system: 1–5 in three different categories.

1. *Atmosphere.* How's the decor? How's the service? What kind of experience do the other patrons seem to be having? Does the look and feel of the place match the food being served?
2. *Taste.* Simply, how is the food?
3. *How do you feel?* Do you feel satisfied? Full? Dizzy? (Yes. Dizzy. It happened once after some fried pies in Oklahoma.)

We now had a system, and suddenly felt like we'd accidentally started an Instagram version of *Diners, Drive-Ins, and Dives.* Which was fine with me because I love that show. It just meant that in addition to all the other ways we prep before heading out on a trip, we now have another line item to check off: finding the right restaurant for the tour. We want variety and local, so we ask online or ask friends from the city. Fairly often the host of the event has a Tour de Tastebuds recommendation for us, but only about half the time is that the one we actually judge.

Last spring we were speaking outside of Pittsburgh, and multiple people had told us the same place—Pamela's—for breakfast. It is also President Obama's favorite breakfast, so that said something to us as well. We arrived in town the night before and didn't need to be at the event until the next afternoon, so Eliza and I got up that morning, put Pamela's into our GPS, and headed out.

As we drove, part of what we were talking about was a really sad text conversation of mine from earlier that weekend, a miscommunication with a man who mattered to me. "It feels like things are falling apart, Eliza," I said to her, "and I'm fine if that's what happens. I really am. It just makes me worry that I've missed God somehow in this." It's that train track thing again, you know? I thought I had some good direction from the Lord of where these tracks were going to go, until things went way off the rails and I was confused.

We turned left to head up a hill, and there, at the top, sat a cathedral. We both gasped and tears came to our eyes. I pulled over on Elm Street and stopped the car right there on the incline, and we stared in silence.

"A cathedral," I whispered to Eliza.

"I know, I know," she said back. "And I know what it means."

———

For months, God kept putting me in the path of cathedrals. I've loved them my whole life actually, but in recent months I couldn't seem to get away from them. In other countries, like Scotland, this is pretty normal. Old churches built centuries ago are around every corner. But in America, not so much. I love them because, more than anything else, they remind me of the history of God.

Here's a confession: I am easily awed. Which is both a gift and a curse. Sometimes it makes me look like a country bumpkin who's never left home for the big city because, "Wow, y'all, look at that!" It means I'm too easily entertained and probably shouldn't be quite so impressed with our planet as I am. "A BUTTERFLY! THAT'S AMAZING!" says no normal person who has ever seen butterflies before. But I do. Often. I mean, did you know during their transformation inside the cocoon, they actually become sort of like goo before emerging? Mind-blowing.

I actually don't mind being awed. I like that I really like life. I like how often I'm just happy to be here and can look for lovely all around me. If you're familiar with the Enneagram, I'm a 7, and we 7s pretty much just love life most of the time . . . or are trying to love it so we can avoid pain.

But cathedrals, for any of us, are awe-inspiring.

Churches are great. I go to one. But my church is a cement box with cement floors. Though it's been our church home for a while, it used to be a storage facility for Goodwill. Cathedrals, on the other hand, never used to be anything else. They were built with a purpose. They continue with that purpose. You never look at a cathedral and wonder what it used to be or what it is now. "Is that a cathedral I see in the distance or an Ikea?"

Cathedrals are monster buildings with minute details around every corner. Tall ornate ceilings, tiled floors, pews, pillars, Latin words inscribed across the walls. Designed in the massive shape of a cross, cathedrals are the way humans have always offered sanctuary and a place to gather to worship an invisible God. They're how we've invited others to come here and believe that there is more to this life than what any of us can see.

They're monuments to God's presence with His people.

People build monuments all the time, to a variety of different things. They all exist to mark a place or a time that doesn't need to be forgotten by the human race. And typically they're accompanied by some kind of historical marker that describes what this statue or building is commemorating.

I LOVE reading historical markers. In fact, walking from my house to my local coffee shop, I pass two historical markers on the sidewalk, and I read both of them word for word every time. It feels mildly insane because DIDN'T I JUST READ THOSE YESTERDAY? But it also matters to me. Someone carved letters out of cement so that the people who lived and did something important in this spot, in this little corner of the universe, would not be forgotten.

It happened in the Bible too. Repeatedly when God rescued His people or healed them or restored them, the Israelites would mark it. Whether with a stack of stones or an altar or a name, they would make a place of remembrance so that God's power and work would not be forgotten. Think of Jacob, for instance—Genesis 32:30—giving a name to the place where he wrestled all night with God. (We'll come back to him later. Mark that too.)

And throughout time, at least throughout the modern ages, the most prominent marking has become cathedrals, which people built to remember God.

———

I walked into Frothy Monkey, a little eatery in the 12 South area of Nashville, to meet our former intern, Sarah, for breakfast. You just cannot go wrong eating breakfast at Frothy. I usually get "The California"–toast and sprouts and avocado slices and two over-medium eggs. I go a little diva and ask for gluten-free toast and a side of crispy bacon. And seriously, it is the breakfast of my dreams.

Someday we can talk about how I used to think runny eggs were the grossest thing in the world until I had these runny eggs at Flat White Kitchen in Durham, England, and they changed my life and I've never been the same. Scrambled eggs are legitimately a memory for me because why would you eat those when you could have eggs over medium? That's where I stand on eggs.

I'd gotten back just a few days before from that trip to Pittsburgh with Eliza. I couldn't wait to tell Sarah how God had shown up, right there on a hill in Pennsylvania. I came in the back door of Frothy and walked up the stairs. The walls inside are decorated with local art which they change out randomly. (Well, it may not be random to them, but it is certainly random to me.) And get this. EVERY picture on the wall was a drawing of a cathedral. YES. FOR REAL. Big regal buildings from around the world.

Sarah was sitting at a table for two along the wall, where a church pew runs the length of the room, creating about seven "tables for two." Sarah looked up at me as I walked toward her. My hand was over my mouth.

"Sarah . . ." I said, almost more a gasp than actually talking. "Look at the walls. It's all cathedrals. How long have these been here? Are they new? Who made them? Is this a joke?"

I didn't sit down. I just walked all around the coffee shop and looked at every picture. A few were labeled "churches" instead of cathedrals, but they had the same look. The same regal build. The same hard-as-stone, not moving, not shaking, survived-fire-and-doubt-and-wind-and-pain look.

God did not want me to miss this. Clearly. He was saying something to me . . . because the heart of this book and the heart of cathedrals seem to be about the same. This may be why God brought the theme to me in the first place. The heart of my struggles involves holding tight to what cathedrals have always meant.

God is who He says He is. Kinder than you imagine. And people have gathered together in cathedrals for decades to be reminded of who He is. That's the only reason those cross-shaped buildings were even created. To remember Him.

When Eliza and I turned that corner in Pittsburgh, and the cathedral rose over the hill, we both burst into tears. And days later, as I sat down with Sarah and looked at the cathedrals lining the walls of Frothy Monkey, tears came to my eyes again.

Because there He was. Again and again. Reminding me to remember Him.

1

I was playing Chutes and Ladders with my five-year-old friend Troy. It's a game I've played for the majority of my life, but knowing how to play doesn't help at all as far as winning goes. There is zero correlation between the time you've put into the game and your chances of winning. Because it is all up to chance.

If it's been a while since you played, here's a quick recap. The game board is a grid of one hundred boxes, ten rows of ten, with each square numbered in order—1 at the bottom right corner, 100 at the top left. All the game pieces start at 1, and the goal of each player is to reach 100 first. Each turn begins with the roll of a single die (or the flick of a spinner), and the number determines how many spaces you move. Throughout the board are ladders that allow you to skip ahead a few boxes if you land at the base of them. But plenty of chutes also appear, causing you to slide back down the board if you're unlucky enough to land on those.

Troy was slaughtering me in the game. I would roll a six and land right on top of a chute, sending me sliding back to the start. Troy would roll a one and get to climb a ladder up ten or fifteen spaces. He was giggling like crazy and trash-talking just as much. I was laughing on the outside, playing along with him, having a great attitude about it. But on the inside? NOT HAPPY ONE BIT. I was super mad, like the kind of mad that almost gives you goose bumps. Anger goose bumps. Yes, they are a thing. *How was this kid beating me?* I have a college education and my own home and I know how to multiply. (He has NONE of those things, can do NONE of those things.) And yet he was killing me.

Webb, Troy's older brother, was across the room from us, doing a Star Wars puzzle. Looked like a good plan to me. I caught sight of Molly, their mom, walking in. She could instantly see how badly I was losing.

"Oh, Annie," she said, "what's happened here?"

Looking up to her from the floor, my face said it all. We've been friends for about twenty-five years, so she knows how to interpret my many and varied faces. "Things are not going so well for me over here," I responded through gritted teeth.

She laughed. That's what best friends do. They laugh at your pain, especially when it's brought on by children and board games.

The game took longer than I wanted—one of those slow, painful board game deaths with lots of twists and turns (eh, chutes and ladders). It ended with him landing on the 100 and then running laps around me, pumping his fists in the air. That's when I decided to write him out of my will.

Troy beat me. It was official.

I immediately started cleaning up the game while he protested that we should go again. I would not. I suggested (insisted) we switch to reading books because, guess what, kid, I know how to read ALL the words. Boom. Sucker.

Later that night as I was falling asleep, I reflected a bit on the afternoon and asked myself a few questions. What had happened there? Why the competitive fire? Why did losing make me legitimately angry when it was all just luck of the roll? Who cares? *And what will you do next time, Annie, to ensure victory?* (Just kidding about that last one . . . sorta.)

I realized something. The reason why losing that game gave me such strong feelings is because Chutes and Ladders is like a picture of my whole life. I saw my story on display there on the floor of Molly's den. It's like we're all playing on the same board, playing against each other, and the rolls of the dice are exactly what they seem—just rolls of the dice. Chance. Luck. Right-place-right-time stuff. I watch you effortlessly roll and get exactly the ladder you want. You climb up and wave down to me. The category could be anything: work, relationships, health, parking spots. Particularly for me, no matter how hard I try to roll so I climb the "husband" ladder, I land on a chute instead, and the dude I'm dating breaks up with me or I want out, and I'm back to square one, literally. I watch as my friends blaze past me on the game board—professionally, personally, spiritually—while I'm just kicking rocks down here on the bottom row. Isn't that just it, sometimes? We feel like what we want has left us second-class to those who've climbed the very ladder we want to climb. Everyone else is winning at life. Us? We're losing.

And in some way, looking around my world at all of my experiences and expectations, they are (wrongfully) telling me something about God.

Steven Furtick famously said, "The reason we struggle with insecurity is because we compare our behind-the-scenes with everyone else's highlight reel."[1] I recognize that's a bit of what I'm doing here. But don't you feel that way sometimes? Like God is the invisible roller in the sky who just drops the dice and says, "Good luck landing *there!*" And as best as you can tell, there's nothing you can do except ride down the chute to a place you don't want to be—all because it was your turn and God tossed the dice.

It's not very kind of Him.

And that's the problem. My problem, at least. This is the core problem of my heart and life that I didn't know how to put into words until Troy schooled me on a decades-old children's game: I know God is loving; I know He is good; I believe He is big and powerful.

But I'm not sure He's kind.

I barely slept that night. A new wrestling had begun, and I knew it. Yes, I'm aware of that Narnia quote of C. S. Lewis about Aslan: "He isn't safe, but he's good." True, but I mostly roll my eyes when people toss that line around, especially when it feels like God is the one tossing the dice.

Randomly over the next few months, I started asking my friends if God is always kind, explaining to them the problem my heart had run into most recently. Once when I posed this question to a respected Bible teacher backstage at a conference, she said, "Oh, sure, well, we often define kindness differently than God does." Then she smiled that knowing Christian smile that says, *"I know it may not feel good or make total sense, but that sentence should make everything okay."* As those anger goose bumps raised on my arms, it took all my self-control not to yell, "DO NOT COME AT ME WITH TWO DIFFERENT DEFINITIONS OF KINDNESS, MA'AM!"

I nodded and held my tongue, but I'm tired of hearing those sentences that are just tweetable enough to make me feel like I'm not allowed to be sad about my life yet leave me feeling that God is sad toward me because I can't just swallow those quips and get over it. Maybe if I could come around to defining words in a way that ensured I wouldn't be disappointed in God—maybe if I could stop asking questions and simply accept my life for what it is—then I could tweet those terrible religious sentences too and get so many RTs it would make your iPhone spin.

But I don't want to do that. I just want to know if He is, or isn't, always kind.

I'm going to do my darndest not to write those cheesy, quippy kinds of sentences here. Because I bet you're as tired of them as I am. I don't want to read or write sentences that only talk about who God is. I want to know Him. Really know Him.

And I want to know if He is kind.

———

Our Bible study started one Tuesday morning on Rebekah's couch. We already had the book to read, *Walk with God* by John Eldredge, about prayer and hearing God's voice.

Five of us gathered regularly to talk and confess and pray, just to find a place to be healed and be quiet and be seen. I needed it. I needed a place where we talked about the Bible and about what God was doing in our lives, but where I didn't have to be a professional Christian. My job—writing books and traveling and speaking at events—along with being the most fun I've ever had, has also done some weird stuff to me, including making me a bit of a secret keeper. It's not that I'm ashamed of things or sinning secretly. It's more that I am incredibly careful who gets to know my business and who doesn't. I lived in full-on self-protection mode for a few years. Often in this self-protective season, if any new friendship started, whoever was sitting across the table from me at the coffee shop would say, "I'm so sorry, I feel like I've talked the whole time"—because they probably had. I learned how to direct a conversation and carry it like an interview. And it wasn't until the very end of the "conversation" that my friend would realize I had only listened and never revealed anything of my own story or my own heart. Brilliant and brutal.

My counselor and I talked about it a lot—how I was able to manipulate conversations so that I offered nothing of my heart. I knew I hadn't always been like this. I used to be an open book. And then I started *writing* books—books that get opened—and my heart began to close. But in this small circle of women during Tuesday morning Bible study, my heart stories began to unlock again.

We would discuss what we had read, and Lauren would lead us through specific prayers. Something would always pop up, a memory or a difficult situation in one of our lives, and we would pray and seek God together for that story, for the redemption of it.

We also ate great snacks.

Our little group gathered a few times a month through the year. And as Christmas came around, some of our dialogue naturally gravitated toward gifts. "Let's not give presents this year," someone suggested. "Let's pray for each other and ask God for specific words to give one another instead."

Now listen. This may seem insane and foreign to you, and I get that. So let me explain a bit. This "asking God for specific words" isn't some sort of witchcraft or weird Jesus-y thing. It's merely praying for someone, then listening to God to see what He would lead us to say to that person to encourage them. The high and lofty Christian term for it is *prophecy.* But no need to hyperspiritualize. It's just listening to God and then sharing what you've heard.

Over and over in the Bible we're told, yes, God is still speaking and we can hear Him. "My sheep listen to my voice; I know them, and they follow me" (John 10:27). "What we have received is not the spirit of the world, but the Spirit who is from God, so that we may understand what God has freely given us" (1 Cor. 2:12). "But when he, the Spirit of truth, comes, he will guide you into all the truth. He will not speak on his own; he will speak only what he hears . . ." (John 16:13). "Whether you turn to the right or to the left, your ears will hear a voice behind you, saying, 'This is the way; walk in it'" (Isa. 30:21). I could go on and on with verses about how we can hear God for ourselves and for other people.

So I sat down that weekend before our Tuesday morning Bible study and prayed for each of my friends. I wrote down each name—HEATHER, for example—and then I prayed for that person. I prayed for what I knew was going on in her life and what I knew mattered to her. I asked God to whisper something to my heart to share with her. Then I sat quietly and waited. For some, a Bible verse would come to my mind. Or a random phrase. Or a picture. And when it did, I simply wrote that down. It didn't have to make sense to me. It didn't have to be something I knew would be incredibly meaningful. I just tried to trust the quiet words that came to mind when I was thinking of my friend, believing the Holy Spirit of God was guiding me.

When we got to Rebekah's for brunch that next Tuesday, we made our plates of food, then sat down and chatted for a bit, catching up on the busy holiday season. (The fact that anyone shows up anywhere correctly between Thanksgiving and New Year's Eve should be a check in your miracle category. Isn't that just the busiest time for you? I feel like I need a flow chart and a flip chart and a pie chart and maybe about twelve pies to survive it.)

The time finally came for sharing our gifts. Each woman took a turn. Heather was up first, and we all went around expressing our hopes, dreams, and whatever we felt God had laid on our hearts. Every time, without fail, we found some tiny theme woven through the gifts we all brought. At the end of each woman's turn, we prayed that God would keep the words that were truly from Him and would drop the ones that were not.

Then it was my turn to listen. My journal was already in my lap, since I'd used it to write down the things I wanted to share with each woman. I grabbed my pen and got ready.

One friend said it was my year to go "IN," take everything deeper—relationships, work, me, and God. She said it was time for me to just really dive in and have no fear. That felt really true for my story, and I was grateful. The next friend said something about proclaiming who God is, not downplaying His power or His words. *Okay,* I thought, *that's cool. I can do that.*

Then Lauren, instead of just sitting there like the others had done, actually stood up and paced back and forth for a few seconds. Finally she stopped, standing behind the couch, facing me from across the room, and looked straight into my eyes, as if this would be hard for her to say, and harder for me to hear.

"This is the year you find *love,*" she said quietly. "I don't even want to do this to you. It feels unfair. But the more I prayed for you, the more I knew that's exactly the word. You don't have to seek it; you will stumble upon it. It will be real. And you need to be able to receive it."

I was stunned.

I wasn't sad, of course.

I wasn't exactly thrilled either.

I just looked at her.

"What?" I asked, not because I didn't hear, but because I wanted to give her a chance to clear things up and tell me more of what she meant.

"I know," she said, never taking her eyes off me. "Trust me. I went back and forth with God, and I know your word is *love*. And you will find it."

I dutifully wrote it down, next to Lauren's name, and then began to look at the theme of what was coming together for me, as for others. This would be the year, my friends were believing, when I would dive in, find love, and proclaim God's kindness. My gift words all wove together. They all made sense. And as my friends prayed for me in that moment, they asked that I would not fear disappointment, that I would live with hope, and that we would see God fulfill what we believed He was saying. *Love* was my word for the coming year, and we believed He would do it in the next twelve months.

Hearing their words and their prayers, I knew something had been conceived in me—a hope, a peace, a joy, a trusting. A new thing had been planted like a mustard seed and would grow. I knew my friends were right. I was supposed to live wide open and available for the next year and watch as God did the thing He said He was going to do.

Y'all know me. *Of course* this was the hope of my heart, to fall in love, to meet the right man who would be an amazing addition to this already extraordinary life I get to lead. I'd believed for a long time that God was going to tell a miracle story with my love life. A few chapters had already been written, story lines I could see Him building for His glory. This would just be the next chapter. I was outwardly thankful, polite, and reserved toward Lauren and the girls, but inwardly I was so full of hope I could have burst.

Love? Whew.

Maybe this thing about love shook me so deeply because it showed up in line with another important word that had come into my life a few months earlier. Each year on my birthday, I ask God for a word for my year. I know lots of people do this at New Year, but I'm more self-centered than that and tend to think the calendar revolves around when I entered into the world. Obviously. ☺ That summer, the morning of my birthday, sitting at a picnic table in Leiper's Fork with my Bible and journal, the word "BRIDE" dropped into my heart. I panicked. Full-out panicked. The fear that God wouldn't come through for me, mixed together with the cost of believing this might be Him really speaking, scared me. I said out loud, "Please don't play with my heart, God, just say anything else." I slammed my Bible shut and hopped up from the table. But the word never left me.

Then here we were, just a few months later, and Lauren was speaking the same theme over my life. It took my breath away.

We get a choice in moments like these. Dive all in, believe no matter what. Or don't. But I also think there's a middle choice: the "believe it, but let it be confirmed, and invite some people into it" spot. Sort of the old "trust but verify" thing. I try to live in that space as much as possible. I want to be full of faith and believe. I really do. I want to remember God even when my circumstances don't always match what I cognitively know about Him. But I also want people to live in my stories with me and help me handle well the voice of God in my life. Both are important. I told the "bride" word to my counselor and a close friend, but that was it. And now, in front of five other women, Lauren was confirming a word she did not know.

My spiritual antenna was *really* up now.

This story is very personal for me, hard to share and almost too revealing. But I need to share it with you, because I need you to know my life changed course that day. My season shifted. Those words from the women who knew and loved me and had listened to God on my behalf set me on a believing path that changed my life.

I knew what I was called to do. And that's honestly what it felt like: a call to believe that God would do what He said He would do. I knew what God was asking of me, especially with the voices of others in this story. I knew what my friends had asked of Him and what they'd heard because of it. God wanted me to believe what I could not see. To trust His words and His provision, and to trust that what wasn't from Him would fall away. To believe that what was from Him would stay and plant in me, and that something would grow.

———

The Enneagram is my favorite personality assessment. I get why someone might feel a bit uneasy about it, but it's actually an ancient method of self-understanding with its roots in biblical thought. According to this system, I am a 7–an *Enthusiast*–meaning, a person who loves fun and does not prefer to face pain. Part of being a 7 also includes being a storyteller, which sure is true of me. I love finding the story line throughout whatever is happening in my day-to-day life. Looking back through my family line, I see its strong power and pull on me from long ago. That's why this book, and each of my books, probably reads more like a novel than those of many other nonfiction authors. I see God first in stories, particularly in the story I live every day.

I want to tell you this story about my life, a story I'm still living but one I've seen coming for a while. And I want to remind you of something: God is incredibly creative, and every story He tells is different. I need you to know this. Not just know it in your mind but know it in your heart, in the very middle of you. Because otherwise, here's what we're likely to do with our stories. (And I still do it myself sometimes.) We see our stories as a game of Chutes and Ladders. We look at the lives of people around us and wonder if we're all on the same playing field and we're getting left behind. I wonder if God remembers them but forgets me. He ladders them and chutes me.

I need us to throw that game board away and see ourselves playing a different game—not *against* each other, but *alongside* each other.

My mom loves to play solitaire. I remember watching her deal out the cards and stack them just so. She would play a lot at our lake house in North Georgia. Her deck of cards in the '80s had purple and red hippos on them, with tiny flower patterns on the hippos' backs.

I loved those cards. They remind me of my childhood. Even just the sound of cards being shuffled is soothing to me. It takes me back to late nights when my sisters and I would be in our twin beds on the screened-in porch, and I would be reading a book by flashlight. My parents and grandparents would still be awake, reading and playing cards. We didn't have a television there, so we relied on every other form of entertainment available. And as I would fall asleep, I'd hear the cards being shuffled on the Formica kitchen table.

Some days when I call Mama, I can tell she's playing solitaire when she answers the phone. She plays on the computer now, but it's her favorite game still. Which, by the way, I actually don't trust computer games because THEY get to decide which card is next, versus the random shuffle of a regular deck in your hands. Technology cheats, y'all. And you can quote me on that.

The goal in solitaire, you probably know, is to stack all the cards in their suit from ace to king. But you start out with them shuffled and then dealt out into piles. You're then allowed to stack them in alternating color, descending in value from king to ace, until the aces are all found and brought to the top of the playing area, where you can build on them from there. You're constantly working, looking, thinking, reconfiguring. You're not just rolling stupid dice and leaving it all up to chance. Nor are you racing everyone else to the finish, declaring winners and losers when you're done. Think of it instead like this: we're sitting here together—you, working with the cards dealt to you; me, working with the cards dealt to me, trusting that the God who deals my deck of cards has done the same for you.

That's more of what I think is happening here.

And as we do, our true stories begin to develop. Yours. Mine. In all their uniqueness and reality . . . like that day at Bible study when it seemed a new stack of cards had started to form in front of me, where I could see them, and so could other people.

In my bedroom is a plastic tub full of journals from the last twenty years. I'm quite the journaler during most seasons. I talk a lot, I write a lot, and I tend to journal a lot. I don't run out of words, for better or for worse. But ever since I was a senior in high school, I have jotted down, in spurts or *en masse*, the stories God was telling in my life, the way the deck was being dealt for me. They're all there—the miracles, the heartbreaks (which either turned out to be rescues or turned out to be pure heartbreak), the tragedies, the joys, the changing of seasons, and the moving of time. The faithfulness of God.

If we could all bring our tubs of journals to the same party—out on the same solitaire table—they would be so different. No two would be the same. Different covers, different spines (spiral only for me, please and thanks). And even if by some crazy chance we'd purchased and written in the same journal, the words inside would be different words, in different handwriting. No two journals would be the same.

I have three beside me right now, the three that have lived with me throughout these last few seasons of my life. I usually finish one and then end up putting it away pretty quickly. But this hasn't been the case lately. Lately I'm flipping back through them frequently, reminding myself of what I knew then that maybe I can still know today. And as I flip through, I thank the Annie from the red floral journal for all the ways she believed, and I thank the Annie from the black and gold journal for not giving up.

I haven't behaved perfectly in my life, and I'm not proud of every word I've written in every journal. I feel like, as my friend Bill Lokey says, I've done some things, in some of my life, rather clumsily. But when I look down into the mess that's now twentyish journals stacked with no rhyme or reason, lying on top of each other, seasons mixed and mingled, I feel sentimental for all the versions of Annie that are represented in there and for the way they've all blended together to make me.

I want you to feel sentimental about you too. I want you draw some hearts around your own life too. I want you to look back on your life—in pictures or journals or knick-knacks—and see that you are you on purpose. Yes, you've experienced some tragedies. Yes, you've been treated in ways you didn't deserve by other people. Yes, hurt exists amidst all the growth and joys and season change. Of course it does. I wouldn't pretend otherwise.

I'm downplaying none of that. I'm not asking you to remember your life with rose-colored glasses. I'm just asking you to remember your life is yours for a reason. For a purpose. And the same is true for me.

I'm also asking you to believe in miracles. I should probably tell you this up front because it'll be woven through here, page after page. I believe in a God who still does the unbelievable in our lives and on our planet, things we cannot understand. I've seen it in my life. I've seen Him do what I did not know He could or would do.

Everything I have been through, even this story, is serving a purpose that future Annie will look back on when these three journals that are sitting beside me end up in the container with the rest of them.

This is my deck of cards.

This is my box of journals.

This is my pew in the cathedral.

This is my story of remembering God.

2

As my books and my life tend to do, we return once again to Scotland.

I grew up in Georgia in a church tradition where babies are christened not long after their birth. So that was my baptism story for many years. I don't remember it, but the pictures and the parents summed it up well for me. Long, off-white christening gown, water dribbled on my feather-haired head, carried down the center aisle of First United Methodist Church by Pastor Sineath, posed politely with my parents afterwards for a photo op.

I made my own public confession of faith years later, but never chose to be baptized, feeling confident that once dribbled always dribbled.

A few decades later, in 2008, I was about to move to Nashville, Tennessee, from my lifelong home in North Georgia. (You can read all about that in *Let's All Be Brave* if you want.) But a week before the moving truck made its way north to Tennessee, I made my way WAY north, and east . . . to Scotland.

It was my third year going there as part of a team from my church who ran a summer camp for middle school and high school students outside Paisley. I couldn't wait to meet up and spend the week with friends who had become like family from the host church, Potter's House, in Stewarton. Our American team was full of teenagers from our church youth group as well, students who only the week before had been at our summer camp in Georgia, being filled up by God's presence and healing. Now here they were, ready to serve students just like them.

After camp ended and all the students and leaders had gone home, we had a few days left to clean up and see some other parts of Scotland. Marie-Claire, one of the high schoolers from home, mentioned in passing that night at dinner that she'd been thinking about getting baptized, same as a few of the Scottish students had done on one of the last days of camp in the small pond at the back of the camp property.

I sat quietly when she said it, but my chest felt like it was going to burst. I was an adult now obviously, but I wanted the same thing. For a few months, the word, the idea, the decision, had randomly circled around in my brain like a sky-writing plane.

Baptism.

I knew I'd been christened as a baby more than twenty years before, but I wanted to do it for myself, to affirm that my life belonged to Christ. His death, His resurrection. I wanted this decided mark in my faith life—a split between what I knew and what was unknown—between leaving life in Marietta and leading into life in Nashville. This baptism, this old life dying and a new life beginning, this washing of my soul and body, this renewal—I wanted it. I knew it was a *Selah* moment happening in my life.

Selah is a word from the Bible. We aren't totally sure what it means, but we know why it is used. Any time the writer of Psalms uses it, it signifies a time to pause and process, to think, to prepare for what is *next*. An empty space that has purpose. And when Marie-Claire brought up baptism, I heard *Selah* for my life.

And what better place than in Scotland? A place that I truly hoped to live someday, where I had so personally experienced God, and where I felt uncannily at home and at peace. (And I just accidentally typed "at HOPE" instead of "at HOME," and it made tears come to my eyes because, yes, there is *hope* there too.)

Once camp was cleaned up the next afternoon, I asked our team leadership if there would be time, I wondered, for a few American students to be baptized (and, you know, one American adult as well). Our Scottish leader/tour guide/chef/dear friend Harry said, yes, in two days' time we'd be at a lake (a "loch" as they call it) where he knew we'd be able to do that.

Loch Ness.

NO JOKE. I was about to be baptized in Loch Ness and hoped that Nessie, the infamous Loch Ness Monster, would let me live to tell about it.

Justin Boggs, one of the trip leaders and a lifelong friend, along with Tom Fraley, a church-planting pastor who was moving with his wife to Edinburgh, Scotland, walked out into the water first. It was freezing. Truly ice cold. The air temperature probably was only about fifty degrees, so the entire situation was NOT WARM AT ALL, but that did not deter us. One by one, the students walked out into the water, where Tom and Justin prayed for them before baptizing them. I watched as each one would be fully submerged to where they almost disappeared, then brought back up out of a ripple of waves.

I was last to be baptized. In the most special turn of events, my cousin Jake and my mom were both along on this trip too, so Jake videoed while Mom took pictures. I walked out to Justin and Tom. These two men meant a lot to me, and it was all I could do not to just burst into tears as I walked deeper toward them into the incredibly cold water. I wanted to memorize every detail. It felt so special—so *Selah*—so once-in-a-lifetime. I wore yoga pants and a long-sleeved green camp shirt. (Sorry, I hadn't brought a swimsuit with me because WHY WOULD I? SCOTLAND WATER IS FREEZING! I had zero plans to get in it.) I reached them, turned around and faced the shore, and clasped my hands in front of my chest. Tom stood to my left and Justin to my right, both with one hand on my back.

Quietly, Tom asked if I was ready. I looked him in the eyes, and through chattering teeth, I said, "Everything changes now, doesn't it?"

"Yes," he said, "it does."

And then he prayed.

And then Justin said, "We baptize you in the name of the Father, Son, and Holy Spirit." I leaned back into their arms, they lowered me into the cold water, and it surrounded me with such force that I thought my chest would collapse. Then as quickly as I was in, I was out. The water that had rushed around to cover me rushed away from me as Tom and Justin pulled me back up. I gasped for air. I can't explain what was going on inside of me except to say I couldn't distinguish between my body being shocked by the cold and my spirit being shocked by His presence. God's provision.

Selah.

Everyone was silent. It was weird actually, because with each of the other baptisms, people cheered right away. But with me, they just stood there. I breathed. Eyes closed. I kept gasping for air, kept needing more oxygen in my lungs.

And I knew it. Everything had changed that day. Something had happened to me. I was marked. God filled an empty place in me that I didn't know was there. He filled it with Himself, and sealed it under a rush of Scottish lake water.

———

Our yoga class this morning used all Justin Bieber music. (I know. It's legit the most fun class ever.) I'm not great at a few of the moves, mainly the extended leg squat that is approximately as awkward and challenging as it sounds. I mean, throw "squat" into any story and I'm gonna want out. But Emmy is a good teacher and keeps us moving fast enough that I don't really have time to leave the room before she's released me from said squat situation and let me return to something less, well, squatty.

My brain spins during these classes. In ways that don't happen during b.fab.fitness (because the music is pumping and I'm dancing so hard), lots of thoughts bubble up as I'm practicing yoga. I try to connect with God throughout, praying, thinking, listening, while also sweating my tail feathers off and trying not to fall over because please, Annie, don't be the girl who falls over during yoga class.

I thought about a lot of things today during yoga. I thought about the first few verses of Romans because that's what I read this morning before class. I thought about how unwise I'd been to come to yoga on an empty stomach because I was starting to feel sick. I thought about the Nashville Predators in the Stanley Cup Final and how my nails were painted navy and gold because I was ALL IN on these guys and their quest for a championship.

Toward the end of class, Emmy had us lay on our stomachs, stretch our arms out to either side, and do some rolling to stretch our shoulders and back. And in the background, Justin Bieber started talking over the music that was playing. Something about trying to "be the best," wanting to be "good at something," and how you "sometimes disappoint people," but with God, "He's perfect and He never disappoints."

God never disappoints.

It stuck out to me. Those few words rolled around in my mind as I rolled around on my yoga mat. Do I believe Justin Bieber? Here I am, sweating my guts out and stretching muscles I didn't know I had, wondering about my life and my story, and running head-on into the same question I can't get away from: *Is God kind? And if I really embrace that, believe that, will I end up disappointed?*

As I walked to my car after class, I thought, *I keep hearing the same question, but I don't know the answer.* And that's true. True-ish.

> I do know the answer.
> I know God is always kind.
> I know He provides.
> I know God does not disappoint.
> But why do I forget what I know?

> Because life isn't always kind.
> And my life doesn't look the way I
>   thought it would.
> And provision has a lot of faces.
> And sometimes I'm really disappointed.

That's the story here. That's what this one is all about. And I'm really glad you're here because this seems like a story we were always meant to live together. If you've been around the block with me a few times, either in books or from a stage or podcast or whatever, then you know me. And you know I wrestle. You know I wish things were easier and wish our stories were more streamlined and tied with a tighter bow at the end. I struggle so much when my expectations of God don't meet the reality of my current experience with life. The sadness has gotten so dark a few times, the loneliness so palpable, that it's made my chest ache. The tears have felt so hot on my face that I wasn't sure my little heart could take the disappointment it seemed to keep experiencing.

But you also know I'm not a quitter and I will not walk away from this book until we are all convinced, myself included, that God is kind—until our belief is ruthless and can stand up against any situation—until we are sure, deep down in our guts, way farther down than where it can be stirred and messed with by life, that God is incredibly kind.

Because He is.

God does not disappoint. He always provides.

Selah. That's what is true, and that's what is swirling around in my mind. The empty places and the things that fill them. The manna, the divine provision from God. The way He shows up in places and faces that we would never expect. This is the part of our God, the kindness part, the show-up-ness part, that's been messing with me. And changing me. And holding me.

If only I can keep from forgetting it.

I can seem to remember the moments, all the major events. But do I remember the truth?

3

Brad and Nan took me out to lunch when I was in Atlanta for the Christmas holidays. Their wedding is the first one I remember attending at our church over twenty years ago, and they both have been fairly regular voices in my life. Brad is the big brother bear who would protect me from anything, given the chance, and Nan is the older sister who listens deeply, loves others really well, and irons her sheets, which was always such a big deal to me. (And rightly so. That's impressive.)

We sat down at West Cobb Diner a little after the lunch rush. Tables were empty all around us except for messy plates from what had once been midday meals. We ordered, small-talked, caught up, and were having a blast. They began to tell me about a marriage conference they'd attended with some other couples from our church in Marietta. I didn't think much of it, except that we were just buzzing through some highlights of life since the last time we were together.

Ever-oh-so-casually, once their recap was finished, Brad mentioned that not only does this organization conduct marriage conferences, but singles conferences too. "Uh huh," I said, clearly and immediately not interested.

"I don't really go to those, you guys. You know that." I reminded them of a few things:

1. I say NO THANK YOU to perfecting my singleness skills by being trained at such a conference.
2. I travel to conferences for my job, so it's not often what I choose to do for fun.
3. I'll never be able to fit it into my schedule. (What I should have said is I'll never ATTEMPT to fit it into my schedule.)

I just was not going to do it. I appreciated lunch, I was so glad to see them and hear how the marriage event had helped them, but I was absolutely not interested.

Just another uncomfortable holiday moment, brought to you by Annie's life. Don't worry, I'm used to it.

Christmas isn't fun for me like it used to be. It's slowly become this ticking clock of a reminder of how, here we are again, and how I promised myself last Christmas, "NEXT year will be different. Your life will be so different. You'll be in a serious relationship FOR SURE by then, Annie." And yet. Tick tick tick boom. Nope. November and December, that little holiday window, tend to mark for me the passing of time, another circle around the sun, another Christmas morning waking up at my parents' house, alone in my bed. Another Thanksgiving meal to mark another year where I show up alone. It was infuriating a bit, and heartbreaking a lot, and something needed to change. Someone needed to rip the hands off the clock in my heart telling me that midnight had struck again and yes, again, my dreams had become pumpkins, not carriages.

Sorry, I was just properly OVER IT that day with Nan and Brad, two days after Christmas, the very day I was driving back to Nashville to get ready to celebrate New Year's Eve. I was tired of being in my hometown for the holidays and not being in my grown-up Nashville life where I feel like the best version of myself, the version I like, the version I want to be.

I'm more sad about what I don't have when I'm in my hometown. I don't totally know what that's about. I think it has to do with expectations and what my life would be if I were still there. I think it has to do with suburbs being mostly families while my life in the city part of Nashville is more balanced. Maybe it's the streets I've known for so long or the bed I still occupy alone on the top floor of my parents' home. Whatever it is, I'm always happy to visit, but always ready to leave.

As we said good-bye from lunch, my heart began to exhale. Time to go home, back to the life I had built in a city that doesn't hurt so much. And Brad and Nan were the perfect ones to send me off. But not without a quick little nudge to my heart.

"Why don't you just check out the website of the conference, see if there's possibly a date that would work for you?" Brad said. And because I love him and because I knew he would ask later if I'd done it, I agreed to do just that and that alone. I would simply look at the website that night when I got home to Nashville, say no, and go to bed, ready to start a new day and a new year.

That night back in Nashville, after dinner with my friends, and after unpacking, and after starting a load of laundry, I sat down on my bed with my laptop open. Just quietly, more to myself than to God, I prayed/said/whispered, "Hey, if this is going to work, it'll need to be really easy and really clear and in a city where no one will know me, and it will need to fit my calendar." (You know, not bossy or bratty at all.)

So I scrolled through the list of approaching dates for the conference. And there was this one. This one in Virginia. It started on a Sunday night and went through a Wednesday afternoon, and I was already speaking that weekend in a different part of Virginia. This one I could easily drive to, this one that was in a quiet little town I'd never known before, this one I could make fit in my schedule and budget.

Shoot. Brad and Nan were going to win. I was going to an entire workshop about being single. About a painful, gaping, incredibly empty space. Woof.

———

I arrived at that church in Virginia, and snow was on the ground, even though it was April. I stayed in an Airbnb just down the street from the church with a married couple who made coffee every morning and prayed for me. They didn't tell me they prayed for me, but I could tell they did. I felt it.

The conference was three and a half days long. The first night, that Sunday, I walked in and people were hubbub-ing around. Many of them knew each other, it appeared, and I was the stranger from a faraway land. I found my name tag and took my seat. In all honesty, I walked into the sanctuary, where the chairs were all in circles, and pretty much determined in my head I had made a mistake. As I sat in my assigned circle, staring at my phone like everyone else, I wondered how in the world Brad and Nan had talked me into this and why in the world I was sitting here. You know that feeling? When you're in a place you're legitimately not sure how you got there because—didn't you swear up and down a few months ago that no, you were not going to attend said conference? *How in the world did this happen,* I thought.

And if I left, would anyone care? Would God care? Because I was ready to go already . . . and the thing hadn't even started yet.

There were eight chairs in each circle, and in the middle were workbooks and pens and a box of tissues. I rolled my eyes immediately. *Nope, they aren't getting tears out of me. I know how to sit in a group and participate without engaging my heart, and I will be doing that here,* I thought. I was going to be there in body, but not in soul. Obeying the word of the law, not the spirit.

The conference was different than anything I expected. We spent more time talking in our group than listening to someone from the front. There was no worship. No darkened room with a lit stage. No fog machine. No altar calls or matching T-shirts or merchandise tables. There was a little teaching and a lot of listening and praying. But I didn't want that. I wanted the darkness of a big room full of people who couldn't see me.

I just didn't want to go there. You know what I wanted? I wanted to sit there and be infused with truth and healing, but I didn't want to participate at all. I didn't want to risk and be open and vulnerable, but I did want to be healed. Thinking back on my baptism in Loch Ness, I wanted the empty to be filled and healed without ever getting into the water. I didn't want to talk to this group about the questions my singleness was making me ask about God and myself (but mostly God). Mainly, HOW IN THE WORLD DID WE GET HERE? That's what I wanted to ask Him. I didn't want to talk to strangers about my heart issues. I wanted God to do right by me.

But it doesn't work like that. Last week when I was playing with the Barnes kids, six-year-old Ben's hand got slammed in a door. It was just a sliding pocket door to the playroom of their house, so while it didn't break his fingers, and while the door wasn't slammed quickly or with extreme force, it certainly popped them and crunched them a bit. He freaked out, as to be expected. (I would too.) He clutched his little injured hand under his other arm and would not, under any circumstances, let me see what had happened. He was crying, wailing, but he wouldn't let me see his fingers to assess how bad the injury really was.

Why do we do that? Why do we do that with our bodies and with our hearts? Why do I do that constantly with God and with other people? Just like my little friend Ben, I'd rather hide my hurts, my empty spaces, even from those who can help heal and fill.

And sitting in that circle of strangers at this conference about singleness, I wanted to keep my injury tucked away, where no one would see it or touch it, possibly causing more harm than good.

But on that first night, they asked us all to pull out our injuries. This room full of singles in all sorts of ages and life stages—never married, widowed, divorced—and they asked us to trust each other, and trust God, that just maybe this was a place where we wouldn't focus on our pain, but we would allow ourselves to be healed.

In general, you know, it starts with a sentence, admitting you have an injury, a pain, an empty space. It can be the hardest thing in the world, to say that one first sentence, send that one first text, make that one first call. But it was hard to walk into a freezing cold Scottish lake too. And at the conference, it started just like that. With a few sentences. Everyone took a turn, I felt the Holy Spirit push, and before I knew it, I was saying the real things.

I didn't get a chance to keep my heart out of the story. I'm just not built that way, which made it more painful than I expected. Not the tears, not the worries, not the people, just the words. To face my history, some of my mistakes and shame, and confess it to practical strangers, the stuff you haven't confessed to trusted friends—it's terrifying and scary and emptying. It was the kind of pain, the kind of empty, that had me in the McDonalds drive-thru after the first night, ordering chicken nuggets.

Now listen, if there is one "uh-oh, Annie is in a bad place" food, it's nuggets.

From McDonalds.

So as I sat in the floor of my prayed-for Airbnb basement apartment, scarfing down nuggets and fries and REAL COKE, yes and amen, I realized something deep was going on. Something that caused me to feel empty, like I needed to be filled.

Though I had tried with all the gusto in me, the first night of this singles conference had flung me into the desert and I was already parched. It pulled me from a place where I was hiding, and it exposed me, like a lone wanderer in the middle of the Sahara. It felt like all my guts were laid out right there, in front of God and those seven people and me. And we all got to inspect them and decide what to do with them.

And it didn't stop there. It was two and a half days of digging into my story and my history and my heartbreak, and listening as the seven people in my group did the same. I said things out loud to those people that I never wanted to say to anyone—stories about my body and sex and men in my life (past and present and hopefully future) and all the things I heard in my head.

I *hated* being there. It was uncomfortable and uneasy. Like a ripping. Or a drowning. Or a shredding.

And then . . .

Something turned. It wasn't a sharp turn. It wasn't like one moment was hard and the next was easy and then we floated away on clouds and butterfly wings. But there was something freeing about opening my heart to the people in my circle, to ask the questions I'd been afraid to ask, to say out loud the pains and worries I'd tried to suppress. They had tapped into something deeply painful in my heart. And they made a place for the Holy Spirit to heal it.

The emptiness didn't disappear. Yet I was able to see it more clearly, see it for what it was. A place that God saw too, all along. God handed me gifts in that church sanctuary, sitting in that circle with seven single strangers who knew more of my trash and secrets than some of my best friends. And I saw His kindness in the empty. I saw His promises in the unknown of my future. I saw His ruthless pursuit of me, even in my pain.

I saw what Christmastime Annie had felt immune to needing, sitting across that lunch table from Brad and Nan, hoping my "no" was coming through loud and clear enough. And actually, I'm glad it didn't. I'm glad my "no" wasn't bigger than God's healing "yes." I knew God was working all these things together, asking me to be brave, even in pain, to walk toward the better He knew I really wanted. This was going to be my year of love. It would be unknown, perhaps, but not empty. Not this time.

4

Lauren's words from Bible study walked through that holiday with me. I got back from Christmas at home with my family and packed up all the holiday décor in my house. I kinda go all in with decorating for Christmas—I just love it. I want a tree and a nativity scene and a mantel with greenery. I want candles and twinkly lights and the whole nine yards.

The only downside is the cleanup. Breaking down all the decorations feels like it takes twelve times longer than putting them up. But I have the plastic containers all labeled and I know just what goes where, so I put on a movie (usually a Hallmark Christmas movie because I LOVE THEM even when Christmas has passed) and I clean, clean, clean and get ready for the New Year.

I love those last few days of the year, when it feels like a fresh start is just around the corner. I try to go through my clothes and shoes and give away any that I don't think I've worn enough to warrant the closet space. I make a stack of books to give away or sell at the local used bookstore. I do a deep clean of every room and get things straightened up and ready for the year.

I think that's a normal thing to do when the seasons are shifting. When summer comes, you know to pack away your sweaters and pull out your shorts. I see my mama friends do it all the time on social media, posting how they're putting their kids' long-sleeved shirts into bins with the size labeled on the side and pulling out summer clothes, ready to be worn and played in.

My friend Rachel is about to have her second baby girl. I was at her house for dinner a few nights ago, and as we walked by the pantry she told me her plans for that week included cleaning and organizing this pantry space. She was going to label the shelves and move things around, go through the food and make sure the expiration dates hadn't passed, and line everything up to make that little pantry right. I smiled and laughed to myself because, wow, I guess NESTING IS SUCH A REAL THING. The pantry absolutely did not need to be organized before the baby arrived. They wouldn't be eating any pantry items for quite some time. But Rachel felt it was very important. So I supported her and promised to do all I could do to help her organize the cans accordingly. I'd seen all my mama friends do this too, getting the nest in tip-top shape so everything is ready when the new baby arrives.

It is super normal and part of the deal, not just for mothers but for all of us. When we know a season is changing, we act like it. We seem to be really good about it in our homes and in our closets and on our calendars, knowing a new season is coming.

But why don't we do it intentionally with our *spiritual* lives? When the winds blow and things seem to be shifting, when something new feels like it's just around the corner for us spiritually, why don't we prepare for it?

———

New Year's Eve was a relatively quiet one. A few girlfriends and I went to a concert of '90s hits, rang in the changing of the calendar, and were in the car on our way back home before the midnight hour was over.

But I knew there was something about this year. I knew I needed to believe Lauren. I needed to act like I knew the season that was coming my way. Faith is being sure of what you hope for and certain of what you can't see, right? Hebrews 11? And so I wanted to believe what the words were saying to me, what God was confirming in my heart. This would be the year. That I could trust Him. That it wasn't my job to do anything except believe and prepare.

So I asked myself the question: If I got exactly what I wanted tomorrow, how would I want to live today? If I knew the season was going to change tomorrow, how would I want to live the sunset of this season? If the empty spaces were soon to be filled, what did I want my days to look like leading up to it?

Just like packing up Christmas and getting ready for the winter, I wanted to get ready for the next season of my life. I wanted to trust and believe that God would do what He had said He would do, and I wanted to trust it as hard as I trusted winter would lead to spring.

———

There was this time once, when God talked to me about the ending of a season. Things were shifting in my life. Unbeknownst to me, I was only weeks away from hearing the first whispers of moving to Nashville. I lived in Kennesaw, Georgia, and had what I thought was the life I would always have—hometown, home church, teaching job at the local elementary school, small group with my lifelong best friends.

Then one day I was praying in the shower (something I often do, as it seems to be a very good place for me to hear from the Lord), just talking to Him about my life and how much I loved things seeming to be so settled and not changing. (Insert crowd laughter here.) And this little whisper came to my mind. It sounded like God, and the whisper said, "When your life changes, you and I change too."

Not that *God* changes. (He never changes.) But He and I, this relationship He's created with me—I should expect to see changes within that.

I chewed on that for a long time. When your life season changes, so does every relationship, and this includes your relationship with God. So before I even knew the depth of the change that was about to happen in my life— leaving everything normal I listed above—I knew this time I was entering was something to savor, just me and God. If everything changes, how do He and I change?

It's been almost a decade since that conversation in the shower, and I still quote it all the time to myself: "When your life changes, you and I change too." It grounds me here with deep appreciation for the season I'm in with God, and it gives me permission to prep for the next one.

———

The church where I grew up was a great church. In fact, I can still tell you how every hallway turns and where the craft supplies are, what the handbells sound like when they hit the cloth-covered tables, and how to sit up straight when you're performing in the massive singing Christmas tree.

And I can tell you how to Lent.

Lent is the season that starts on Ash Wednesday and runs until Easter. So it's a February to April-ish thing, as a rule, and the intent of it is to help us to deal with feeling the loss, the sacrifice, the pain of our sins, the quiet of the heartache of Christ.

Growing up Methodist, I started "giving things up for Lent" about the same time I started attending youth group. I gave up chocolate. Coke. TV. You name it, if it even had a hint of smelling unhealthy, I found a year to give it up. This pattern didn't change as I entered college and got super involved with the Wesley Foundation, the Methodist student ministry at the University of Georgia. I kept observing Lent. And at that point, as most things go in college, it wasn't because my parents or church made me. I wanted to.

Something happens when I observe Lent. *I feel it.* It moves me. The forty days stretch me and hurt in the middle. I feel the pain of it every year. And I want to quit repeatedly, but I know Easter is coming.

That's what Lent is meant to bring about—an absolute celebration of Easter morning. All the sacrifice and the waiting is over. Jesus is risen. AND YOU CAN EAT DESSERT AGAIN. Praise hands go up everywhere.

Richard Rohr says Enneagram 7s like me have to remember that Good Friday happened and not just Easter. We love fun and try to avoid pain, like I've said, so skipping over the worst day to get to the best day feels pretty on-brand for the way I'd like to live if I chose to be an unhealthy version of myself. But observing Lent is a great way for me to connect with pain instead of run from it. (And still get REALLY excited when Easter comes.)

I've kept observing Lent as I've grown up and moved to Nashville. (Or, moved to Nashville and then grew up, because that's how it feels like it happened. But that's another story for another time.) Lent started in February, and I was ready for it.

I had this feeling at the start of Lent that the season was changing and I wanted to know more about God. As much as I could learn as quickly as I could learn it. Not that He was leaving or anything, but—again, when seasons change, so do He and I. Ours is a serious, committed relationship, a friendship that I want to be the nearest and dearest in my life. And because it is a real relationship, it has hard times and good times and times when we need to relearn each other a bit. (Clearly me doing the relearning here because, hi, He's God and He knows everything.)

So I decided my Lent experience that year needed to be about learning God, especially because this year felt really pivotal and like it was ushering in change. I wanted to double down on the God I knew and the God I wanted to know better. More time, more focus, more understanding, so that when things did change, I'd have known

Him the best I could during the season in which I'd most recently been.

My goal, every day of Lent that year, was to write down one thing that was true about who God is to me. So I opened my iPhone and started a note: "Who God Is to Me." I committed myself to list, every single day, exactly who He is to me and who He had shown Himself to be that very day.

I was strong then, in the winter. My new book was about to come out. It was good, I thought. Maybe very good, they told me. And it would do well, maybe very well, and this might actually be when my professional life would change. We were just a few months into this promised year, this year where the tide was going to turn in my job and in my life. I'd already written about my love life in *Let's All Be Brave* and *Looking for Lovely*, and I knew whatever I wrote next was going to tell a different story. I was full of faith and hope and certainty . . .

Except for the whispers. The cracks in the cement. The little place where something wasn't right. I barely saw it, but I saw it enough to know that making this list of "Who God Is to Me" was necessary and good. I was going to need to remind myself who God was and who He is and who He specifically is to me. Because somewhere in the back corner of my soul, I was really afraid I was going to forget. I didn't know to articulate it at the time. I only felt the cracks. But now I realize just how much I needed to make that list.

So every day I looked for God. I was intentional about trying to see Him because I knew if I made a list, I would see Him working in my life.

Though I'm an avid pen-and-paper journaler, I made the list on my phone because I wanted to have it with me at any point in the day. Any time I felt the nudge of God's character coming through in a situation, I wanted to note it. I wanted to look for Him in the anywhere, versus just seeing Him in my morning time of reading the Bible or in church. I wanted to look for Him in nature and in friend-ships and out the window of airplanes. So having the list ready with me at any moment really mattered to me.

I started my list on February 10, almost two months to the day after our Bible study breakfast, two months into remembering what God had said about this year.

Day 1 / February 10 = He is the God who holds me

I was on the road, driving home from speaking to col-lege students in Kentucky. I was sad. I was lonely. And I needed to remember He truly wraps me up and holds me close.

Day 2 / February 11 = He is the God who orders my steps and watches my calendar

Again, a road life problem. I was drowning in travel and speaking events. Having to carry all of that responsibility made me feel exhausted and deeply alone. But I knew God was seeing every step. So instead of panicking, deep breaths. Breathing in. Sighing out.

Day 3 / February 12 = God is always available to listen to me

And it went like this for the next forty days, missing a few here and there, especially toward the end. With a new book releasing and travel becoming hectic, I began to wear down. I could feel it in my core, in the very middle of me. Who I knew God to be and who I needed Him to be were still not matching up. I couldn't find His kindness anywhere as the Lenten season came to a close. In fact, for as hard as I was trying, I was struggling to find Him at all.

What is happening here, I wondered, *and who am I becoming?* It didn't feel like things were going right. But I didn't know why. Or what to do about it.

5

I put the fancy bottle of bubbly in the fridge that morning before I left for the office, hoping I would be opening it hours later. I had bought it from Schramsberg Winery in Napa Valley, California, for one reason: to be opened the day my book hit the *New York Times* Bestsellers List. And we really thought it could be today.

I got home from work and sat on the short brown couch against the wall of the living room, under the asymmetrical print I purchased years ago. It was 5:30 p.m. on an April Wednesday. This was when we would find out. Had *Looking for Lovely* sold enough copies to be on "The List," as we call it? Publishers receive The List on the Wednesday before The List actually comes out on a Sunday, but not until the end of the business day in New York. My agent, Lisa, had told me to expect a call from her between 5:30 and 6:30.

I hadn't bought this couch. It was free. Adam and Ansley gave it to me when they were redoing their house, and they knew I needed more seating for my Tuesday night college small group. Its multicolored, woven strands appear in various shades of warm: red and brown and deep yellow and hunter green. The room was dark. I'd forgotten to turn on any lights when I got home from the office, and spring was just picking up. The days were still cold and short. I plugged my phone in beside the couch and sat down right in the middle.

With my legs crossed under me and my phone in my lap, I said, "Everything changes today, one way or the other. It all changes now." (I'm realizing for the first time, I'm fairly aware of the moments when that phrase is appropriate. Baptism. *New York Times*. Every new single dude who enters my life.) I knew if my book hit The List, it could be a career changer. And I knew if it didn't, I'd walk a long journey until the next opportunity. We'd come very close with *Let's All Be Brave,* and missing The List had been a heartbreaker. So I already knew the feelings of not hitting. And I knew how long I'd waited to be sitting here on this couch, waiting for news one more time.

Because here's the thing. Making The List isn't the be-all-end-all of all the things. It's just a list. It changes every week. But in our industry, it's one of the things that determines who's the best. It puts your book in front of a lot of people who may not otherwise have known it existed. And that's what mattered to me. That's why I wanted to be on The List. Wasn't it?

Just once, I thought. *I want to hit The List just once. It doesn't even need to hit high. I'm MORE than happy to take the last slot.*

I just wanted a slot.

I kept thinking about who I would call first. We'd done all the hard work to make sure my friends knew the book was out and make sure they were equipped to tell their friends. More people than I deserve had posted about the book on their social media and told their followers to buy it. We watched the book not only climb up sales charts but stay there. Every. Day. Of. That. Week. Even my friend Rusty, who's an expert in the business and just plain doesn't lie to me, had called on Friday before the sales week closed Saturday night, and said, "I seriously think you've got this if you have a good push today and tomorrow."

Rusty knew what my whole team knows: I like to win. I like to set goals and achieve them, and I had my eye on that prize of hitting The List. Not only that, it felt important to my story. This book that had asked so much of my heart was destined to be a winner. I'd earned it, right? We'd strategized for months. We'd done all we knew to do. And I kept hearing Christine Caine in my mind, saying, "God puts books in hands." So I asked Him to do just that. *Put this book in all the right hands. Don't let one hand miss the book that's supposed to hold it. And toss it in a few extras so there's no denying a spot on The List.*

Shelley Giglio said to me one time, "We are so good at preparing for failure that we don't make plans that prepare us for success." So I dreamed big and made plans for success. I really believed we'd get it. Statistically, we knew we were extremely close to success. I just knew it. We'd done it.

So as I waited, I thought about what I would do if we hit The List.

I would wait ten minutes after my agent called me. For ten minutes I would sit there and be the only person in my world who knew we'd done it.

Then I would call my parents.

Next I would text Haley, Molly, and Misti, my best friends from home.

After that, I would drive over to Dave and Annie's. We'd smile and cheer, and the kids would jump around even though they didn't totally get why, and after the spontaneous party we wouldn't know what else to do, so we'd move on to their news from my news.

When I left, I would text our girls' group text and see who was up for dinner, and when we got there, I'd say, "This is on me. It's a celebration. Because my new book is a *New York Times* bestseller." (And then I'd be in debt because, by the way, you don't make any money for being on The List.)

So with my legs crossed and my phone in my lap, I kept side-eyeing the clock that hangs on the wall above my fireplace, doing nothing but wondering what it was going to feel like when my fifth published book became a bestseller.

5:35.

5:52.

6:03.

6:17.

6:25.

YES! A text comes in.

Lisa Jackson:
Just heard: we didn't hit.

Annie Downs:
Shoot. Okay.
Shoot.
Hate that.

Lisa Jackson:
Not for lack of trying though, that's for darn sure.

Annie Downs:
Shoot. That's so sad.
How did we miss? Ugh.

Lisa Jackson:
I know. I really wanted this for you.

Annie Downs:
Pulled the fancy champagne out of the fridge. Save it for another time.

Lisa Jackson:

You have so much to be proud of. You had a fabulous launch week, and this book is going to do really, really well. Trust that.

Annie Downs:

Did we make any of the other ones you were watching? Shoot. I hate this.

Lisa Jackson:

I haven't seen any new lists released yet. I'll keep my eye on them.

Annie Downs:

Okay. Well. We tried.

Well. We tried.

And failed.

I didn't drink the fancy champagne.

Ricky Bobby, that wise sage, once said, "If you ain't first, you're last," and dang if I don't agree with him. I sure felt it at the time. I didn't care how many books we sold that first week if we didn't sell enough to be on The List.

Again, an empty space that God could have filled, but He didn't.

———

I didn't call anybody. Luckily, I hadn't gotten anyone else's hopes up on a Wednesday (everyone thought we'd know about The List on Sunday), so I pulled my iPad onto my lap from the corner of the couch and began to play a game. Cooking Fever. My best little five-year-old friend Parker and her sister Sloane had introduced it to me and it was fun enough, so I played for a few rounds.

And then I got off the couch and got ready to leave. Alton Brown, possibly my favorite chef ever, was doing a live show that night at the Tennessee Performing Arts Center, and my roommate, Amanda, and I had tickets. So I changed clothes, freshened up my makeup, grabbed the tickets and my purse, and hopped into a cab to head downtown.

Not a tear. Not a thrown book across the room. Not a screaming fit.

I just kept shaking my head and saying, "Shoot." Over and over again.

But the life emptied from my eyes. I could feel it. I could fake it fine watching Alton Brown do science food experiments while I ate caramel popcorn, but I knew everything inside me was turning from the life-pumping shade of red to a lifeless gray.

———

The next morning, I couldn't wake up. My alarm went off and I silenced it, rolled over, and kept sleeping. I slept until almost 1:00, even though I'd gone to bed before midnight. When I was finally groggily able to pull myself out of bed, I thought, *Man, I must have needed this day off pretty bad.* I ate some lunch and could not keep my eyes open. So I laid back down, took a two-hour nap, and then met some girls for dinner. By 10:00 p.m., I was exhausted again.

No one outside of my publishing partners knew we hadn't hit The List. My friends and family didn't know. But I was devastated. I was so devastated that I felt numb. Nothing felt like anything because nothing mattered. When I thought about God, I thought about nothing.

THIS was His doing?

THIS was the best He had to offer me?

THIS is what I got for pouring my guts into a book because He asked me to?

And, by the way, I still had no boyfriend or dates to even speak of. Where was the LOVE that I'd been promised back in December? Was it all just a cruel joke—this whole trusting God with my life and believing with all my heart that He would show up like I thought He would?

HELLO, GOD.
IT'S ME, ANNIE.
ARE YOU OUT THERE?

Gray. All I felt was gray.

And all I wanted to do was play Cooking Fever.

But I couldn't stay awake.

And it wasn't just about the book. You see that, right? The book was nothing but a highly visible, public sign that said I'd done all the work I knew to do, truly exhausted myself (and my team), then trusted God with the rest, but still it hadn't been enough. And when I plugged that sentence in to my life, it's like it lit a strand of bulbs I could trace throughout my faith journey, where I felt like I'd done my part but God hadn't. And it broke my heart.

For the days that followed, I was a shadow of myself. I didn't eat; I couldn't stay awake during the day; I couldn't fall asleep at night. I faked it pretty fine for most of my friends, but Eliza knew. My roommate, Amanda, knew.

Cooking Fever took over all my free time. Do you know about it? It's an incredibly fun game on your iPhone or iPad. You open restaurants and earn money by serving customers quickly and correctly. The game starts with a simple burger and hot dog joint. I got to be a pro and passed all forty of those levels fairly quickly. (Yep. Forty.) Then with the money you make, you purchase other restaurants. And the forty levels continue with each restaurant you open.

Sounds fun for about twelve minutes, right? I played for hours at a time. Literally hours. I laid on the couch in the dark, or in my bed in the dark, and served up hot dogs, hamburgers, fries, milk shakes, Chinese cuisine, pizzas, you name it.

I felt like a person I didn't even know.

I had never felt so tired. And no matter what I did, I couldn't shake it. I couldn't take enough naps or sleep in enough days to counteract whatever was going on in my body. That was what scared me, I think. It wasn't that I was having all these negative sad thoughts. It's not like I was crying myself to sleep. I wasn't doing that at all, actually. Instead, it was more like my body folded in and simply gave up.

Listen, I'm not a quitter. I used to be, but I don't quit anymore. You can read all about that journey in the *Publishers Weekly* bestseller (but so far NOT The List bestseller) *Looking for Lovely*. But it was an insane thing for the release of that particular book to be what caused my body to quit. I mean, it totally gave up and just went limp on me. I couldn't bring myself to exercise more than about once a week. Where walking the trails at Radnor Lake had become a really important place for my heart and body, it was now such a chore.

I was still traveling and speaking at events during this time. But I would land in the city of the event where I was speaking, go to the hotel room, and be in the bed until I had to get ready. Then when I absolutely HAD to get up, I would calculate, down to the MINUTE, how long until I could be back in that bed. I would say to myself, "Okay, Downs, you can do this. It's only five hours and thirty-five minutes. That's it."

One night, after returning back to the hotel from speaking, I peeled off my clothes and slid into pajamas as quickly as possible, pulled my hair into a top knot, and sat down on the bed. My head in my hands, I was thinking about the next day. It was a two-day conference, and I needed to teach again on Saturday morning. I was slumped over myself, hunchbacked, thinking, *This is the side no one sees. I wish there was a photographer here to take a picture. Because no one knows this is happening.*

I looked to my right, where I noticed a mirrored wall I hadn't seen before. And then I laughed a bit to myself, and thought, *Well, I've got an iPhone and a mirrored wall . . .* and took the picture myself.

It looked so depressing. One lamp on, in a generic hotel room, one woman slumped over her crossed legs on the bed, study materials out in front of her, an empty emotionless face.

Something was really wrong in a year when things were supposed to go really right.

———

The next week, my counselor said the word "depression." She didn't say I was severely depressed; she just said that some of these things—the sleeping, the sadness, the grayness, the Cooking Fever—when combined all together, can be symptoms of a depressed season.

Where. Was. God.

What. Was. Going. On.

Kindness? Faith? Belief? Not only was He not doing what He said He would do a few months back, and not only was He not doing what I had believed He would do, but now my life was actually falling apart even more than ever before! What in the world? This isn't how this year or this story was supposed to play out.

I had never experienced anything like this. Sure, I'd been through disappointing seasons and sad seasons, but nothing that felt this all-pervasive and oceanic. I was so blindsided by it. Here I'd expected to turn the corner into this year and be on the yellow brick road all the way to Oz, and instead I found myself in some sort of swamp that I feared might never release me.

That's the fear I felt.

What if this was the rest of my life?

What if I never came up out of this swamp?

What if something had broken in me and I was never the same again?

Was I supposed to find God and life and joy and His kindness in here?

It all felt wrong. I'm Annie. I'm loud and silly and fun, and I don't have to fake that. But here I was, pretending all the time unless I was home. And when I was home, I was empty.

I didn't know how to survive another month like April. It had been so unnerving and surprising and numb. All I knew to do was to ask God to show up for me once a day. Just once. And I would grab hold of that once a day and breathe deep of it, like it was an oxygen tank.

I made two lists that year.

Well. Let me clarify that. Because the math is actually that I made a bazillion lists that year, such as: what I needed at Target; which of my friends are which Enneagram numbers; the characteristics of my dream house.

I like to make lists.

But I made two lists that I *had* to make. Because I had to remember.

The first was that Lenten list—all the things God was to me. It's insane to think how that little list started out in such a hopeful, strong time and ushered me into the darkness. My journals go quiet for about twenty-five days there, between early April and early May. Dark, dark, dark. You can imagine. I didn't know what to say about anything . . . except Cooking Fever, and I wasn't sure God really cared all that much about the virtual restaurants I was owning.

I decided to get proactive in May about not drowning in my ocean of painful emotions. Depression can't really be handled like that. I know that now. But it was my first rodeo with this particular bull, and I thought there was a real chance I could just muscle my way through and pull myself up and out.

Again on my phone, I started a note titled "You're Gonna Love Maaayyyyy," because I have so much love for NSYNC and that one particular Justin Timberlake meme, so I switched "It's Gonna Be May" to "You're Gonna Love May" and would sing it every time I opened the list. On May 1, I typed out each date—May 1 to May 31. And I told myself, "Annie, whatever it takes, you are going to find something great about every day. You are going to look for God and look for beauty and make the choice to see good in every day."

May 1 was a Sunday, and some friends and I had tickets to a Sam's Place show at Ryman Auditorium. I believe the Ryman is one of Nashville's greatest treasures. And this particular show—Sam's Place—connects right to that.

Sam's Place happens on Sunday nights, a few times a year, usually in the summer. It's a variety show hosted by Steven Curtis Chapman that celebrates the roots of the Ryman. The evening is named after Sam Jones, the preacher who came to Nashville more than a hundred years ago and ushered in a revival. It's why the Ryman exists today—because in 1885, a Nashville riverboat captain named Thomas Ryman heard Jones speak at a tent revival downtown. Sam Jones preached about Jesus and saving grace, and it changed Ryman's life forever. The two men began to dream up a gathering place for all the people who were giving their lives to Christ. First known as the Union Gospel Tabernacle, the building opened in 1892.

I think about this all the time—how our city saw real revival 130-ish years ago, and how our whole downtown is sort of shaped around this building that was only erected because people needed a place to worship. I think about how much I want God to do it again, and how cool it would be if it started in that room, and how we still get to worship there too sometimes, in the pews that once held droves of new Christians. Amazing.

It is a cathedral, of sorts.

So on Sunday nights, Steven hosts a little throwback to that time so we can gather today, think of God, think of Sam Jones, and hear some incredible music. Whenever the audience is invited to sing along, the *a cappella* voices rising from the pews will bring tears to your eyes. The air buzzes with the feeling that something special started here, and if we just sit long enough, we'd get to feel that thing again.

On this particular Sunday night, our tickets were in section 10, almost all the way to the right of the balcony. Fifth or sixth row, great view of the stage and of the room in general. The Ryman is shaped like a half moon. You can look across from one side of the balcony to the other and see just about everyone on your level and the one below as well.

I was happy to be there, relieved a little bit because that's how my heart feels in the Ryman. But I was sad because my heart didn't feel like itself and hadn't in awhile. Getting myself ready for the evening had been a real fight. I had timed how long it would be before I could be back in my bed (four hours and nineteen minutes was my best guess). But I had to go. Because for the first time ever, my friend Hillary was performing songs with her family from her gospel album.

When Steven brought Hillary out on stage, the crowd went wild. Many people know her for being in the country group Lady Antebellum, but this was something new. She moved to the center of the stage, in a fierce one-piece black jumpsuit, and began to sing "Thy Will."

It was a song she had sent me a few weeks before . . . before April, before Cooking Fever. And I had tried to listen to it as often as possible during those hard weeks. I believed its lyrics would infuse into my heart somehow.

We moved down to the empty first row of the balcony as the piano played. Hearing those words sung
"live" for the first time—about knowing we've heard Him,
knowing we've followed, only to be left confused and
brokenhearted, clinging to those four words: "Thy will be
done"—they melted me.

Again, I was crying. And it felt like God and I were
meeting for the first time in a lot of days, right there in the
Ryman, where He's met with a lot of others throughout
the generations. The Holy Spirit just knows how to move
in that room because He's moved there so many times
before. I thought about my list for May—finding something
great about every day—and I knew this was Day 1: Hillary
singing "Thy Will" at the Ryman. In a season where
beauty was incredibly hard to find for me, one of my best
friends singing truth over me held me together that night.

I woke up on the morning of May 3 with a song in my
head. It happens sometimes. Not every morning. But
when it does, particularly when it's a worship song, I pay
attention. (To be fair, I woke up today with a Spice Girls
song in my head, so I didn't dig too hard into the meaning
behind that.) On May 3, while I was smack in the middle

of the grayest season I had ever known, to wake up singing a worship song was unusual.

I trust it, though . . . because sometimes I think my
little soul can do a lot more worshiping when my mind
isn't involved. So even while I'm sleeping, I pray for my
inner Annie to connect even more deeply to God. It's not
spooky or weird; I just want all of me to rest. So when I
wake up singing a worship song, I figure my insides may
have been singing it all night long.

I couldn't get the song out of my mind, a Bethel Music
song from the *Have It All* album called "Spirit Move."

And, oh, how I wanted that to be true. *Yes, Lord. Won't
You come and move on my behalf? Please? It feels like I'm getting
eaten alive every day. Could You come?* I just kept singing the
lines of the song over and over, asking God to "ride in"
and "rescue" me. It's something I say frequently—how
Jesus saved me once but He rescues me all the time. And,
by gosh, I was in a place where He could prove it. *Prove
that You rescue me, God!*

Once I was ready for the day, before heading to the
office, I went and sat on that same warm-toned couch,
right in the middle, and I wrote out the entire song in my
journal. Every lyric. And I told God, "I feel it in my bones.
You are about to move, aren't You?"

And just that minute, something happened to my
body. I'm going to explain it the best way I know how,

knowing it may sound loony to you. It was like whatever darkness had been pressing on my shoulders suddenly lifted. My neck started to hurt, as if I'd slept with my pillow turned the wrong way. And my legs were suddenly sore, like I'd been running a race. Then my stomach got upset and I had to run to the bathroom. No kidding, it was like my body had been held captive and was suddenly released. I've never experienced anything like it.

Everything was sore, but the thing that caught my attention was that I was crying. Not weeping, not sad, but tears were just rolling down my face, as if my body was making a whole lot of healing choices but wasn't involving my mind at all. And I knew I was free. Whatever had held me for weeks was gone. I had been a captive (more than I realized, I think), and there on that little couch, on a Tuesday, I got rescued.

It doesn't always happen like that. Healing isn't always immediate and miraculous. I know people who have wrestled with mental illness for decades and people who have died from cancer. I've seen deaf people be able to hear in an instant and people who didn't know God existed experience Him personally, altering their lives forever. I don't understand healing and how it works. I don't think there's a magic word or a certain way to sit or stand that moves God to answer in one way or another. I just know in this one story in my life, God's kindness looked like an immediate escape hatch opened for me. In one sitting, in the same place where it started, it finished. It was gone. The demonic forces at play were no longer welcome on this playground.

I wouldn't have believed healing could happen so instantly if I hadn't experienced it in my body like I did. But on May 3, everything suddenly changed. My soul had been baptized again. Not *into* something, but *out of* something. I could tell. And it marked me forever.

———

I kept my list going the whole month, even after the rescue came, and it just about blew my mind. Little things caught my attention I'd never seen before. Moments that held no significance for me ordinarily were bringing tears to my eyes because of God's kindness. Big things that could just as easily have happened any other time all seemed to line up for me in May.

A few examples:

> May 2: *Looking for Lovely* was nominated for a book award.

> May 6: The bookstore in my neighborhood posted my name on their huge sign, saying I was the author of the month.

May 9: Did the first of a few really fun speaking events.

May 10: My speaking agent gave me a miniature tour bus with my face plastered on the side because he knows that's my dream someday. (Ridiculous, I know. But I just think it would be hilarious.)

May 13: *Looking for Lovely* hit a bestseller list. And it happened again on May 17.

May 15: A tiny, beautiful baby was born in Texas to some dear friends of mine.

May 24: Our interns started work, and we were immediately the best group of friends ever.

May 25: I took a really long nap.

All of this great stuff happened in May, after I hadn't made THE List but started making *my* list.

And on May 25, after taking that long nap, I pulled out my phone and wrote down the whole list by hand. I did it because His kindness had been manna for me, in so many different forms and places and faces. I did it because I'd felt His rescue in a deeper and truer way than I could ever have expected. I did it because sometimes healing is immediate, and that's certainly God's kindness, but sometimes healing doesn't happen like we picture it, and somehow that's God's kindness too.

————

Just this week I sat in my counselor's office and told her all about how I'm feeling now that this season is a bit behind me. Despite being warmed and encouraged by some invigorating shafts of light, I can never again be the woman who didn't experience that darkness. I can never say I haven't felt depression's grip. I can never forget what those middle-of-the-night bouts of numbness felt like. I can never go back to her, to that Annie who didn't know the surprise of deep darkness.

This darkest season marked me forever. It's done a thing in me I can't explain, except that I keep picturing what happens when a chunk of stone gets chipped out of a statue. It doesn't ruin the statue, but it sure does change it permanently.

And that feels like me. I can't pretend I didn't stand out in the storm while my entire self got soaked and beat up. I can't pretend my soul hasn't been weathered. It has. I'm rougher for it. I'm chipped forever. I have a limp that will not heal.

Yet maybe . . . maybe . . .

Maybe the limp *is* the healing.

I think of Jacob in Genesis 32 when he wrestled "a man" (clearly, from verse 28, it was some form or expression of God) and refused to let go of Him until He blessed Jacob.

> Jacob was left alone, and a man wrestled with him till daybreak. When the man saw that he could not overpower him, he touched the socket of Jacob's hip so that his hip was wrenched as he wrestled with the man. Then the man said, "Let me go, for it is daybreak." But Jacob replied, "I will not let you go unless you bless me." (Gen. 32:24–26)

In John Ortberg's book *I'd Like You More If You Were More Like Me*, he writes, "When the struggle is over, Jacob is left with a limp that—as far as we know—never went away. He wanted a blessing, and he got a limp. Or maybe the limp *was* his blessing."[2]

So here I am with a limp, and it has slowed me down. It's caused fear and caution in places where I didn't have them before.

May was better, yes. Borderline great. Incredibly thankful for that. But still, my expectations for the year versus the reality of the first few months were incredibly hard on me. Harder than I knew. Hard enough that even now, long after the wrestling has passed, I still feel the sting, I still feel the tension from it—*I still walk with a limp*— even though God has proven to be every bit as faithful as He promised.

I suppose, then, I'm expected to look at everything on balance and call it His kindness—that maybe part of *keeping* my spiritual balance comes from limping forward through whatever season comes my way.

I woke up on a Friday morning and heard a whisper in my heart.

Fast for a week. For revelation.

It was June, just two weeks before my birthday, just a month after the rescue of late April and May, six months after Lauren's word about my year, and I had been asking God to say some things to me. I needed clarity as my next year on the planet was ending.

The word for my year, the word I received on my birthday, the one I told you came just before our Christmas words, the word I knew God was saying to me, was "bride." Woof. Brutal. What a terrible word to think you hear from your God to define your year, especially a word so deeply connected to your most prominent pain point (and hope point). But I had believed Him. I had written it down and remembered it. Then Christmas happened, and Lauren said this was my year to find love, and the words paired together almost TOO well. Yet here I was, the next summer, very single indeed, with two weeks left until "bride" ended, and that word didn't make a lick of sense to me. I'd been on dates with a few men here and there, but nothing that stuck.

To be fair, the word did make some sense with the year I had. God had prepared my heart for Him in so many ways, Him being God Himself. I grew and changed so much in that year that I could see how He was making me ready. While I hoped for a husband, I knew so much of the preparation was for Him and for where we were going.

So God and I had been ping-ponging that around for a few weeks. I wanted to understand. But other things were going on too. Things deeply personal that were mostly just my heart asking if God heard my prayers. So to wake up and recognize His voice and have Him ask for my focused attention for the next seven days felt special. Kind. And really interesting. Never before had I felt like He was just leaning down out of heaven over my sleeping self, waking me up and whispering straight into my ear. But I knew it. No doubt. I don't claim to have a red phone to God, but I do know His voice most of the time. I've been in a relation-ship with Him for a lot of years at this point, and just like with every other relationship I'm in, the longer I've known the friend, the better I recognize the voice of my friend. I knew what I had heard.

Fast for seven days.

And look for revelation.

This was an important detail for me because so often when we fast, we're looking for things to change. We're looking for an outward shift. But this felt like God was more looking for an inward thing for me. I was supposed to be watching and listening to see what He was about to do. And this was important to me because I didn't want to fast in order for God to fix the "bride thing," as I had come to label it. I just wanted to listen to Him, now that it felt light again, as if some color had returned in the few weeks since the lifting, replacing the grays of a brutal spring.

A seven-day fast? I hadn't done that in years.

In fact, the last one? When I lived in Scotland. (Of course.)

It always points back there. The thread Scotland weaves in my life is as thick as a ski rope.

The last time I had fasted like this, we were asking God for direction, the leadership team at Crossroads Church in Edinburgh. Fasting is great for that—giving you focused time, encouraging your heart to do some spiritual planking for the sake of what you need or want from God. For us, it was a need for guidance in how to reach and make friends with university students. So we went in hard for seven days, fasting and praying.

Fasting isn't as bad as it sounds except IT IS. I'm not going to lie. Not eating is the pits. Day Three is particularly hard for me. It's something about your body being like, "Those first two days were cute and all, but *hi!*—I want food," and then starting to yell expletives at you from your insides. Not good.

But actually, it is really good. On one hand, it empties you. Literally. But then there's also this thing that happens when you fast, some would call it a special grace. But to me, it just feels like God leans in. It's not a manipulative move on your part. You aren't fasting to keep Him paying attention to you. It's just biblically true that He is moved by fasting and prayer.

I looked at the calendar on my phone that morning, and, amazingly, I had the quietest week possible. One dinner on the books, and that was it. Huh. It might work after all. I thought back on that week in Edinburgh when we fasted as a team, and I texted Tom Fraley, my pastor from there—the same one who'd baptized me years before—and I asked if he could FaceTime me in the next few days. He said he'd be available to chat in about an hour.

Well. Things were certainly falling in place for me to do this thing and be very hungry for the next week. Again, interesting.

Tom and I hopped on a call that afternoon.

He was in the car, waiting on his wife, Leigh Ann, as she shopped for groceries. I was in my car as well, outside a Nashville coffee shop, between meetings. We did the simple catch-up things, and then I laid out my situation.

I didn't need Tom's permission to fast. I knew what had been whispered to me. I needed his leadership and covering as I entered into it. And I needed to have someone know I wasn't doing this to GET something from God (though at times that is totally appropriate). I knew that wasn't the goal here. The goal was for me to connect and listen and receive revelation.

> *Revelation:* a surprising and previously unknown fact, especially one that is made known in a dramatic way

Well, that certainly seemed to line up exactly with what was going on here. This definition felt really sweet to me. God wanted to tell me some facts—things that are indisputably true—and make them known to me in a rather dramatic way.

I told Tom all that was going on with me. The bride thing, the love thing, what I felt like God had whispered to me that morning. I knew involving Tom had to do with the purity of my heart. I didn't really want to do this, to fast for a week just before my birthday. But I definitely didn't want to be deceived into seeing it as a power or manipulative move toward God, and I needed some accountability to stay true to that. There are times when fasting for a change is exactly the right thing to do. That wasn't now. This was clearly about God sharing something from His heart with me, and I needed the focused time and clarity that comes when I'm not concerned about how the over-medium egg is cooked on my avocado toast from Portland Brew or if I get enough yellow sauce with my fries at Burger Up.

Tom listened, gave me a few wise words about fasting well, reminded me of some Scriptures that I needed to focus on, and prayed. And he told me he believed in me and knew I could do it, and that he agreed this was important.

When I got home later, I pulled out my journal to note the things he said. I wanted to record it all, to make sure the details of this thing stayed true and straight for me from the start.

Tom had told me to write down these verses from 1 Peter:

> In all this you greatly rejoice, though now for a little while you may have had to suffer grief in all kinds of trials. These have come so that the proven genuineness of your faith—of greater worth than gold, which perishes even though refined by fire—may result in praise, glory and honor when Jesus Christ is revealed. Though you have not seen him, you love him;

and even though you do not see him now,
you believe in him and are filled with an
inexpressible and glorious joy, for you are
receiving the end result of your faith, the
salvation of your souls. (1:6–9)

I loved it in *The Message* version too.

I know how great this makes you feel,
even though you have to put up with every
kind of aggravation in the meantime. Pure
gold put in the fire comes out of it proved
pure; genuine faith put through this suf-
fering comes out proved genuine. When
Jesus wraps this all up, it's your faith, not
your gold, that God will have on display
as evidence of his victory. You never saw
him, yet you love him. You still don't see
him, yet you trust him—with laughter and
singing. Because you kept on believing,
you'll get what you're looking forward to:
total salvation.

The fast started on a Sunday. It would last until the
following Saturday night. I didn't know much except that.
And I knew God had things to say to me. I had some
questions to bring to the table myself. And I was listening.

———

I bought a lot of juice that Sunday. (No way am I the hard-core type of faster who only drinks water for seven days. I'm guzzling juice like a professional. And when my stomach hurts from the sweet of fruit juice, I turn to vegetable juice. But ewwww. I do not like it.)

In addition to the impressive collection of juice, I made a list in my journal of the topics I was hoping to discuss with God. I felt certain He had an agenda of things, but if I was going to be hungry for seven days, I was bringing my list as well and hope we got around to it.

My list included:

- There was a new man in my life and I wanted clarity
- All the words that people had shared with me in the past six months
- Some family things

I wrote a few thoughts about each of these entries, describing for myself the point of tension surrounding each of them and what I was hoping God would do or say. Then I closed my mouth and opened my ears.

A church I love in town meets on Sunday afternoons and my roommate went there, so I decided to go with her that Sunday. I'd been attending my home church, Cross Point, for about five years, but something felt off there. I often left feeling more drained than filled. This other church was like drinking from a fire hose. And I was thirsty.

We popped in the car in the late afternoon and headed over to where the church gathered. I took along my journal and my Bible and a real sense that these next few days could mean something special to me. That was my preparation to begin what would turn out to be one of the most significant weeks of my life. In a season where I was struggling to breathe at Cross Point, The Belonging was like an oxygen tank for me.

I sat between my roommate and my friend Kelsey. A husband and wife, Henry and Alex, each led a portion of the service. Henry led in worship and then Alex taught the Scriptures. I had heard her before. She's a power punch of the gospel in a tiny frame. I liked her spunk and her love of Jesus.

And right off, she started teaching about trusting God when you're waiting.

I almost busted out laughing. What are the chances I would show up at a church I don't regularly attend on the night I'm starting to fast for revelation, and this person is going on about exactly what I need?

She taught from Romans 4 on Abraham and his faith: "He did not waver through unbelief regarding the promise of God, but was strengthened in his faith and gave glory to God, being fully persuaded that God had power to do what he had promised" (vv. 20–21). And she asked a question I've never forgotten:

> Am I fully persuaded that God is for me
> and He will answer my prayers and fulfill
> His promises?

Fully. Persuaded.

I saw the words on the page in my Bible. How had I missed them before? And how should those words change my life? What did it actually mean for me to be "fully persuaded"? I knew it didn't mean I would get anything I could think up to want. I knew God wasn't a vending machine. But what would it look like for me to be fully persuaded that God is at work? Fully persuaded that He is *for* me? Fully persuaded that He is kind?

"Abraham's faith didn't strengthen him," Alex taught from stage that day. "The knowledge of the God of his faith is what strengthened him." I wrote that down. Yes, it's not about the words we've heard or the promises; it's just about who God is.

After finishing, she had the congregation stand up. And as the worship band began to play, Alex said, "I want to pray for the women in the room who are unmarried and over forty. God is going to do something new for you."

Shoot, I thought, *I'm not forty, but GOSH, wouldn't it be amazing if she meant me?* I looked up at Kelsey (she's a legit supermodel, very beautiful and very tall, so if we're both standing, I'm definitely looking up at her). She put her arm around me. "This is for you too," she said confidently. "We're just going to believe it."

And so I tried, like Abraham, to stand full in faith and open my hands believing that even though I was a few years younger than her cutoff, I could maybe receive some of the crumbs as they fell off the adult table.

Then she prayed, and with open hands I chose to receive it. Surely mid-thirties could steal a prayer for a forty-plus, right?

Fully. Persuaded.

I knew in my gut that God wanted me to cling to this. The entire experience was beginning to feel like a treasure map or a hunt of some sort. Normally when you think of the Holy Spirit, you probably think of the dove that descended on Jesus when He was being baptized. But did you also know that Celtic Christians call the Holy Spirit *Ah Geadh-Glas,* which means "wild goose"? Don't you love that? Because if you've ever tried to follow the leading of the Holy Spirit, for sure it can feel like a wild goose chase.

But I knew the phrase "fully persuaded" was for me. This word from Scripture was part of my wild Holy Spirit chase.

I got home and tweeted at Alex.

> I'm not forty-plus, but your prayer tonight got to the heart
> of me. Thank you. #fullypersuaded

Within minutes, even though I'd never met her, Alex messaged me back. She gave me her phone number and said we should meet up.

And that she'd seen me and thought of me when she prayed that prayer.

8

I woke up that Monday morning, grabbed a juice from the fridge, and then headed to my khaki chair with the black swirls. It's been my spot for years. Like, almost a decade. Next to it is the table that used to be my grandmother's bedside table. It's got one exposed horizontal shelf on top of four vertical shelves where she used to keep the phone books lined up. Now it holds all manner of spiritual books for me: the ones I'm reading, the ones I'm referencing, journals recently finished.

I go through the same routine every morning, a luxury brought about by being single. I wake up about six and go start hot water for my tea. Then I walk through the house opening the curtains, shades, and blinds. Depending on the time of year, this either allows light in or reveals the need to turn on a few lamps because of how dark it still is outside. On this day in June, it brightened the kitchen, my office, the living room. Then, like every morning, I sat in my chair, legs crossed under me, with the brown blanket over my lap, and I read. And journaled. And prayed.

Juice replaced the tea this morning, and I was hungry.

Almost laughable to be hungry on Day Two when you're headed for Day Seven, but I was. My stomach was growling for food. The first few days, your body is so vocal thinking maybe you've forgotten to feed it, and that maybe yelling at you might remind you. My body was acting like a wide-awake baby stuck in a crib.

So in my moment of desperation, I decided to read where Jesus says that man doesn't live by bread alone. If He could resist the temptation of food throughout forty days, surely I could survive the first forty HOURS of my own fast.

I searched on my phone for the location of that Scripture, and then I opened my Bible. I've used the same Bible since 1995, when I was in the ninth grade. My parents gave it to me as a Christmas present that year, *The Quest Study Bible*, because it's the kind of Bible my friend Molly used, and I wanted to be just like her. Over the years, through high school, college, my life as a teacher, my life in Nashville, and my life in Edinburgh, this Bible has probably been the only consistent companion across all stages of my life. The verses that are underlined, the notes out to the side in the margins—they all remind me of this story I've been living for decades now. I see Bible teachers and friends get excited to have a new Bible, and I definitely own other ones of different translations that I reference often. But MY Bible? It's the navy blue one that's already been re-covered once and now is duct-taped again. The edges of the covers are frayed and the tabs have all fallen off. It's more than just words on pages. It's more than just a copy of God's Word to humankind. My Bible is where God's history has met my history, and I treasure it more than any other object I own.

So I opened to Matthew 4 and read the story of Jesus' temptation in the desert, focusing on verse 4 where He said those words: "Man shall not live on bread alone, but on every word that comes from the mouth of God." My weak soul responded by saying, *Oh yeah, Jesus, I so get it. You and me are so similar and so hungry.* (Please insert your own eye-roll here because I am so dramatic and apparently so sure I am just like Jesus when I'm hungry.)

Next to this verse in my Bible is a tiny italic *a*, informing me to look down to the bottom of the page for additional info. All throughout Jesus' temptation in the wilderness, He was quoting the Old Testament to Satan, and this line He said in Matthew 4:4 was first said somewhere else. So I traced my finger down to that little *a,* where I saw a reference to Deuteronomy 8:3, and I turned there.

I haven't spent tons of time in Deuteronomy, but ever since I was a kid I've heard the story (or watched the movie) of Moses leading God's people out of Egypt into the desert for forty years and then on to the Promised Land. In the early parts of this Old Testament book, they're out of Egypt already, and Moses has gathered all the people together to tell them what God had said—how they were to behave, how they were to handle themselves, how they were to live in the land they were about to enter. So I started reading Deuteronomy 8. And here was the part Jesus had quoted. Notice what else is around it.

> He humbled you, causing you to hunger and then feeding you with manna, which neither you nor your ancestors had known, to teach you that man does not live on bread alone but on every word that comes from the mouth of the LORD. (v. 3)

Here it is also in *The Message*.

> He put you through hard times. He made you go hungry. Then he fed you with manna, something neither you nor your parents knew anything about, so you would learn that men and women don't live by bread only; we live by every word that comes from GOD's mouth.

Manna. That's the first word that jumped out at me. Yes, I'd heard this word a lot of times. God's provision. His kindness to the people of Israel while they were out in the desert. Having fled from Egypt with nothing, the people began to complain about being hungry, and God heard them, causing manna to miraculously appear in front of their tents every morning.

The book of Exodus describes it as being "white like coriander seed and tasted like wafers made with honey" (16:31). It appeared six days a week for them to collect. On the sixth day, they were to collect enough manna for two days so that no one would work on the seventh day, the Sabbath. The name *manna* came from their asking, "What is it?" because they'd never experienced anything like this food before. That's literally what manna means: "What is it?"

Like, you'd walk over to your neighbor's tent and say, "We're short half a cup of what-is-it and were wondering if you could share. I promise I'll collect an extra cup of what-is-it for your family tomorrow." So bizarre.

Manna fed the millions of Israelites in the desert, on a daily basis, for a very long time.

People today still use the idea of manna to describe God's provision. Though we don't see actual manna in our yards each morning when we wake up, God does provide for His people. It may not look like anything we've ever seen before, and it may not be what we expected, but it is still His provision. He fills us when we are empty.

I read Deuteronomy 8:3 again. "Then he fed you with manna, something neither you nor your parents knew anything about" (MSG). I was writing the verse in my journal when that phrase jumped out at me: "Something neither you nor your parents knew anything about."

My body's hunger pains stopped, and my heart pains came into clear view.

My parents got married when they were in their mid-twenties. In fact, I clearly remember my mom telling me when I was a college student about her wedding at the age of twenty-six. I thought, "My gosh, she was so old. Surely I won't be that old when I get married."

I was born the same year my dad turned thirty and my grandmothers both turned sixty. I loved the math of that. I always planned my life to be sure I'd have a kid within my thirtieth year—not my first child, since thirty was late in the game. But I would work really hard to have *one* of my children during that year in my life so I could keep the tradition going.

Funny, the expectations we set for ourselves, how we make all these random executive decisions:

- If I don't own a house by the age of _____, I've failed.
- If I don't have _____ by the age of _____, I've failed.
- If my career doesn't make sense or I haven't settled into the workforce by the age of _____, I've failed.

That's what it comes down to, isn't it? This idea that there's a right way and a right time to do something, as well as a wrong way and a wrong time.

When we think like that, we haven't even factored God into the story yet. (How much does He complicate things?) Because meeting a spouse or finding the right house or getting pregnant or being in a job you love—only by His provision do we achieve any of this. They all require Him to provide. But more than just provision, I was expecting Him to be on the same script as me. Honestly—and this is scary to say, but—I thought those dreams were on His script. I thought I was operating with the understanding that we both wanted the same things for me, that the manna He'd prepared would look like a dude and some kids, approximately a decade ago.

But I was wrong. My dreams did not become reality. According to my calendar and my life plan, He really missed the memo. Big time. I'm creeping into territory where my body will not easily be able to do the FIRST time what I was planning on my body being FINISHED doing by now, because I wasn't married by the ripe old age of twenty-six. And don't tell Annie back then, but I also wasn't married by the age of thirty-six. So I didn't have a child at thirty, breaking the three-generation tradition my grandmothers had begun.

I obviously know way too much about a life my parents and their parents know *nothing* about.

Recently I'd started to think about what it would have been like, in the culture of 1952, to have your first child late in life, compared to now. I mentioned to you my dad's mother being thirty when he was born. My other grandmother was thirty-two in 1952 when she had her first child, my mom. Wonder what either of them felt or experienced, not having children until later than many of their 1952 friends?

I grew up across the driveway from my mother's parents. Ma, my mom's mom, was like another mother to us. She was fun and smart and loved to watch me dance to "Lavender Blue" in my purple tutu. I felt a special connection with her, but I always thought it was just because she loved her grandchildren so well. But now, as I'm looking over this math, I'm realizing there's something deeper here that neither of us could have known while she was still alive.

I called my parents one evening to think this through, since they were a little closer to the 1950s than I was. They happened to be sitting around a table with their best-friend couple, and I asked them what they thought would be the modern-day equivalent of a woman in 1952 who was thirty-two when she had her first child. What would Ma have known, I wondered, about waiting, and about life plans not working out, and about how it feels to be RIGHT HERE?

Well, biologically speaking, there's a way to figure that out. My dad, the accountant, started doing the math in his head and talking about life expectancy between the decades. The equation would look like this:

$$\frac{\text{Age when first child born (in 1952)}}{\text{Life expectancy (in 1952)}} = \frac{\text{Age when first child born (today)}}{\text{Life expectancy (today)}}$$

Plugging in the numbers for my particular question, here's the math:

$$\frac{32 \text{ (in 1952)}}{71 \text{ (in 1952)}} = \frac{x \text{ (today)}}{81 \text{ (today)}}$$

Calling on my ninth-grade math skills, I remembered the way to solve for x is simple: $(32 \times 81) \div 71 = x$

$$(32 \times 81) \div 71 = 36.5$$

36.5

Exactly my age.

And I started to cry.

Because it just may be true that while I thought no one understood me, a lot of what I've felt up to this point in my life may be similar to what Ma felt too. Her story was far more complicated than mine—poverty, abandonment, war, divorce—but the math is the math. And while my life is quite different from hers, it's also more similar than I realized. Delayed answers. Unmet expectations. Living outside the cultural norm.

And I wish I could call her today and ask her questions that only two women in this math equation can understand.

———

Everyone wants something they don't have. Everyone can point to a place in their life that feels like a barren wasteland. Even if someone was in their best season ever, and you handed them a microphone and asked, "What do you want that you don't have," they'd still be able to give you an answer. Whether it's a bigger house, or more job opportunities, or greater influence, or kids, or a girlfriend or boyfriend or whatever—everyone I know wants something they don't have. Don't you? What do you want that you don't have?

That's what makes life feel like a *wilderness,* to me at least, which is exactly where the Israelites were located when God provided them with manna. In the wilderness. This entire planet is about wilderness, but God is about manna. The journey of life is not a matter of finding our way out of the wilderness but finding the manna inside the wilderness.

Do you see that? Was I seeing that? We can be in the wilderness *and* be fed. Those two realities are not mutually exclusive. Life can be painful and beautiful at the exact same time. Scripture says He will bring us "into the wilderness" and "speak tenderly" to us (Hosea 2:14). His kindness brings us to Him. The wilderness does not mean abandonment; it means a chance to see this manna that neither we nor our ancestors have ever known. It won't always look the way we thought it would. It won't always look like the family and future we envisioned for ourselves, the kind we hold up as the expected standard. You may even find yourself asking, "What is this? What is it?" That's because it will be *manna.* Something else. Something yet unknown. Perhaps even something much, much better.

Deuteronomy 8. Manna that neither I nor my parents had ever known. True, my parents did not know single-ness in their thirties. My mother, though a lawyer and hard worker, did not provide for herself for twenty years after graduating college. My parents have never moved to another town.

But I have.

And back on that Monday of the fast in June, I sat in my swirly chair just dumbfounded at the idea that God had said, thousands of years ago, He would be for me what other people didn't know He could be. He has fed my heart and soul in ways I didn't know He could do.

———

Women have a yearly checkup at a particular doctor that men do not go to. There's no reason for me to say any more than that, because if you're a woman you know exactly what happens, and if you're a man you don't need to know it from me. But of all the transitions involved in moving to a new city a few years ago, the challenge of switching dry cleaners, churches, and doctors seemed to be the hardest. I hadn't made the doctor switch yet.

I was no stranger to an ob-gyn office, thanks to a medical condition that's given me irregular periods my entire life, so I didn't fear going to one. Obviously it's awkward and uncomfortable, but I kinda had an "eh, whatever" attitude about it. I'd gone to the same ob-gyn my entire life, and now it was time to go to another. So the first summer after moving to Nashville, I asked around, and found that nearly all my friends went to the same ob-gyn.

I made the appointment for a few days before my thirtieth birthday with this woman, Susanna Trabue. My friends absolutely loved her. When I met her, she was smiley and beautiful with a long blonde braid. I noticed immediately she was single (no ring at least), and she looked just a bit older than me. We kicked off talking before the examination started, and it wasn't long until we were talking about the real stuff. She's also a Christian, so once we hit that common ground, there was no going back.

Finally, when the examination was complete, she asked me something else: how I felt about being thirty and single. As much as I'd played it off to myself and my friends, I was suddenly teary. Maybe it was the whole being naked except for a blue paper robe thing, but I felt really exposed. And sad. And surprised to be here, on an ob-gyn's table in Nashville, days from turning thirty and still a virgin, still unmarried, still sorry that this was my story. She patted me on the knee and said she understood. She told me a bit about her life as a thirty-six-year-old single woman and how God had cared for her, even in her disappointment.

I nodded, tears streaming down my cheeks. (Why was I naked and crying in front of this woman I didn't even know?!? UGH.) I believed her, but I grieved my story anyway, which she said was okay. Then she asked if she could pray for me. And I'll never forget this. She said, "Annie, just because I pray for you doesn't mean you're going to end up being thirty-six and single. Don't worry about that."

Which, to be fair, has TOTALLY happened, but in that moment, I remember thinking how selfless of her. What an amazing example of thinking more about me than herself. As if her life was something to be feared or some sort of plague. It wasn't. It isn't.

This may sound silly and dramatic, but I didn't know I could survive and thrive in this life I'm living today in my thirties. I feared this exact story. The story I was so scared would be mine that day is the one I am living right now. That's why one of the things Susanna said all those years ago, besides the prayer, still sticks out to me. She told me all the ways God had been more than enough for her. Had been manna to her. I listened to what she said, and I guess I believed, but I probably didn't. Yet she told me of this thing she and Jesus shared together that meant the world to her. She told me how He'd been exactly what she needed and how He'd also become everything she wanted too.

Zoom ahead now to that Monday of the fast, a few years later, the last one before my next birthday, just two days from my next appointment with her. While journaling about my grandmother and manna, I got it. I got it in my own Annie way—how God had provided manna for me all along, and how more often than not, HE had been the manna. He Himself had been the manna that provided and supplied and held me.

This was *revelation* to me, just like He'd promised the Friday before the fast started. He was showing me what I didn't already know. And man, I did not know all the things He was to me. Even though I'd made that list at Lent, this was different. This wasn't about His characteristics; this was about His heart. This wasn't me describing Him; this was Him telling me about US, about who we were to each other, about all the gaps in my heart He had filled. He had loved me so well for decades, truly, and He fed my heart and my soul. He'd always provided. He'd *revealed* to me a great truth about manna.

And the week had only begun.

9

Every day of the fast I went back to that list I'd created and put in my journal at the beginning of the week. One of those items, you may recall from chapter 7, was clarity about a particular relationship.

A man who'd come into my life about a year before had circled back around, and I was curious. As with any man who came into my life after that December brunch, I wondered. The beautiful thing was that this year, I knew it was the season to expect such things. I knew the right guy was coming. And so if it didn't work out, I'd say to myself or my counselor or roommate, Amanda, "I hate that it didn't work out, but he won't be the last if he's not the right one. The right one is coming. I know the season." And I did. While I felt the sadness whenever a relationship didn't work, I never despaired. I knew the season.

Another topic I really wanted God's whispers about was my body. My relationship with my body is a never-ending roller coaster. It's the most volatile relationship in my life. There's so much love and hate shot back and forth between my mind and my body. Some seasons we work together great; other seasons we fight like mortal enemies.

And after such a weird spring, my exercise and eating had gotten way off balance. Even in my journal, where I'd noted it as one of the topics I hoped we would cover, it was just a quiet side note in hopes of God and I having time to get there.

I won't linger here long. I've written other books that tell all about my story with food and my body and Polycystic Ovarian Syndrome (PCOS). But there seems to be just a core thing about me that probably means this battle will always be happening somewhere within close proximity. The years and the healing and the counseling, along with the hard work of choosing love toward myself, have made it easier overall. But the lies are not silent. The voices have not ceased. And I certainly at times run face-first into walls of self-hatred that leave me dazed and bewildered, with little tweety birds circling around my head.

But can't everyone find something to beat themselves up about on the regular? Either your looks or your brain or your spiritual life or your professional life. Or a combination of two or all or a whole other list of things. Mine just so happens to have been the same since fourth grade.

This body thing.

———

(Never thought I'd write a book where I told of two different ob-gyn appointments, but here we go, and to the fellas out there—love you, mean it, and I'm so sorry.)

I couldn't believe my appointment this year fell the same week as the fast. Except I *could* believe it because it felt really true and right and . . . because *of course* God would orchestrate things that way.

A few years before, when I had come into her office, Susanna had talked to me about my weight. She wasn't condemning or unkind; she just noticed I was gaining. And when you have PCOS, gaining is more than just unfortunate for your closet. It's a sign that your body isn't fighting the disease, a sign that your body is not processing well, and for me it's a sign that I am not doing for my body what my body needs.

A sign that I'm not trusting God.

PCOS can make it difficult to get pregnant. And even though I'm not married, every time He and I would talk about this disease, I felt like God was asking me if I believed Him. Did I really believe He would be kind enough to answer my heart's prayer to be a wife and a mom? If I did, why did I treat my body like I didn't believe Him?

I would pray and journal and tell people that I believed God had that story for my life, but I would eat and exercise (or not exercise) like my body didn't believe God. I knew exactly what I needed to do to get my body to a healthy place to get pregnant, but I wasn't doing it.

I wasn't trying to have a baby; I was trying to believe God. I wasn't trying to get pregnant *that day*, but I was trying to ruthlessly behave in a way that showed my faith. Maybe not to other people, but to me. I wanted to believe God so hard that He is the God who provides, and that He is the God who is kind, that I wanted to treat my body like I was trying to get pregnant every day, even when I wasn't. It was an act of faith, more than an act of health.

I think of Elijah at the end of 1 Kings 18, when he knew it was going to rain, but no clouds were appearing. I knew what God had said to me and the people in my life over the last few months. I knew the rain was coming. There were just no clouds to speak of. But Elijah told the people to party because the rain *was* coming, even though they couldn't even see clouds. I wanted to live my life by the same principle: let's party like God's about to do what we've always hoped (knew?) He would do, before we even see the clouds.

In 2013, God started a healing process in me. I started taking my PCOS seriously, started eating the way I should, began slowly to find exercise I enjoyed. And my body started displaying signs that things were improving, that it was in working order. Every appointment with Susanna turned to joy because we got to talk about healing and faith and what it looks like to believe God even when you don't see your circumstances change.

So when my appointment time came around this year, on this week of fasting and revelation, I was thinking about this little side note in my journal as I pulled into the parking garage. A few minutes later, I was sitting on that table again, less dressed than I like to be when in a public place, and waiting on Susanna to come in.

I knew exactly what I weighed, approximately three pounds less than the year before. It felt a bit like my body was stuck at this one place and, no matter what, it wasn't shrinking any more. I was frustrated (hence the reason this had ended up in my journal in the first place, even just as an aside).

She walked in and we hugged and began to catch up. Then she asked me what I weighed, and I told her.

"Sounds like it's your sweet spot," she said calmly.

I teared up and she said it again. "This is your sweet spot." She told me how healthy my body was, and seemingly my mind, and how she believed I was doing the best by my body that I could. Therefore, she said, this window of weight was what she felt was healthy for me. I may not exactly love it, this number. But for me, she said, it's my sweet spot.

After the appointment, I got back in my car and was just slack-jawed. Sweet spot. I'm in my "sweet spot." I don't look the way models look, I don't love everything about my body, and honestly I still fight it more than I wish I did. But I also needed to trust the truth of Susanna's statement. In the middle of a fast for revelation, in the middle of a week when God said He wanted to tell me some facts I didn't know, this felt like more than I could have even asked for.

———

What if that is the truth of it all? What if I am actually in my sweet spot? Even with the limp, even with the unmet desires and unfulfilled dreams, what if I saw it all as my sweet spot, right where I am supposed to be? This thought has kept spinning around in my mind, even as recently as a few nights ago while I was sitting at a table with my girlfriends.

I don't remember when our friend group started. I should ask someone. Surely one of the other nine girls remembers how this all kicked off. Maybe it had to do with watching television together, or maybe it was when Bailey moved in with Anna and Jen and started baking a lot of bread to share. Maybe it was our Thanksgiving "Friends-giving" dinners each year. But something started a group text of ten single girls a few years ago, and it has never quit.

We've had a few changes over the years. Most excitingly, a few of our gals have gotten married. And you have not seen a dance floor or reception venue ready for the likes of us. We swarm in like bees and have the best time. And now we have a couple of babies to add to the pack since the brides have become mamas.

We've also suffered devastating loss, tragedies, diagnoses, and heartbreak. We circle around each other in those times too. And because Nashville is a bit of a transient town, sometimes people move away. Of the ten of us who originally banded together in this thing, zero were born and raised here. We all moved in at some point, and now, in a slow trickle, we are starting to move away too.

Nashville is like that. New people are constantly moving to town, and sadly, people fairly constantly move away as well. And Sunday night, the nine of us who remain met up at Bella Napoli to say good-bye to another.

Bella Napoli is a tiny Italian restaurant tucked in behind Edgehill Village. It used to be the only thing back in that little stretch of buildings, but now a few other hot spots have cropped up, making it a little more known. You walk down this brick alley with Edison bulb lights strung crisscross down the whole alley to the door of Bella Napoli. If you're lucky and there's an open table and the weather is just right, you can sit outside under the lights. But when it's a breezy Sunday night in June and you show up in a pack of nine, the chances aren't so good for sitting outside. So instead, they sat us in the back room of the restaurant, with just one or two other tables.

Anna was moving away. A new job for her husband in Seattle meant that in just a few short days the moving trucks would be packed, and Kyle and Anna and their puppies would be on their way clear across the country. It felt incredibly sad.

Nashville is like that. Since most of us move here as adults, without our parents or any family, the friends you make become the family you choose. And so for family members to leave is always hard. On this night we sat around a long dark table in a long dark room to say good-bye to family.

We ordered pizzas and split salads and told hilarious stories that had happened since we'd last been together, at Laura's wedding in New Orleans. We talked about TV shows on MTV when we were in college and tried to remember our favorite game shows from childhood. We coupled up and talked in groups a few times, because nine women around a table can't hold one conversation forever.

Then once we'd devoured and picked over the pizzas, once the waitress had cleared our plates and refilled each of our glasses, the mood downshifted.

Here's why we were here.

"What do you need from us, Anna?" one friend asked. "How can we pray? What does it look like to care for you well?"

I was across from Anna, about two seats down, spinning the stem of my glass between my fingers. I stopped, we all did, and looked right at our sister. What did she need from us?

Anna teared up immediately, dabbing her cloth napkin at the corners of her eyes. "I just want y'all to believe that God will take care of you," she said quietly, but confidently, as she looked around the table, making eye contact with all of us. "He will provide for you," she continued, "and He sees you, and He is better than we realize."

I was stunned. And tears were pouring down my face as well, as were most girls' faces around the table. We asked what she needed, and what she needed was for us to believe. Just believe. To see God for who He really is, not for who our circumstances were trying to tell us He is. To believe that here was a sweet spot. To believe this table, these friends, this life, with this God of ours, is sweet.

10

The fast set the pace for my whole summer. Each of those revelations, each of those facts from God to me, spoke something that changed the atmosphere of my life.

I'd become "fully persuaded," trusting (trying at least to trust) God's power to keep every one of His promises to me. I'd been freshly encouraged to seek and receive His provision, His manna, in all the wilderness areas of my life, in ways I'd never known before. Even with questions unanswered and paths unclear and adversities unrelenting, I'd found a sweet spot in simple, sweet belief.

Oh, and I also damaged my eye.

Long story short, I ended up needing LASIK eye surgery to protect myself from further damage and to correct my vision. Dr. Horn, one of the best eye doctors in town, was able to make space for me to undergo the procedure early in the fall. It lasted less than ten minutes. I wasn't scared, but I did get to take a Valium so any fear feelings were calmly soothed by medication.

I cried when they finished repairing my eyes. As soon as the surgery is done, you can see almost perfectly right away, just a few blurry spots, but in general, you can see.

In a lot of cases you can see perfectly clear. That was me. It was the closest thing to a miracle I had ever experienced.

I could see!—20/15 vision. Things that had been visible enough with contacts and glasses were now stunningly crisp after LASIK. I thought I could see great with contacts, but I had no idea what I wasn't seeing. Even looking down at my hands would bring tears to my eyes. I could see details that had never stood out to me before. I could read a clock across the room. I could see the doctor. I could see my mom. The list of things that shocked and awed me that first week was endless.

It changed my life forever. I still, many days, am struck by a moment or two of just thankfulness and wow because I can see so many things, any time I want to see them.

But that day also seemed to usher in the start of a season I didn't see coming. So bizarre to be able to see so clearly, for the first time ever, just in time to watch, clearly, a lot of people leave.

———

I kept hearing "change" all summer long. I knew God was prepping my heart, pushing me that way. I wrote it in my journal a few times. "This fall will bring change." And of course, living fully persuaded and all, I thought I understood.

My healthy eyes were the start. On a Thursday, Dr. Horn changed my eyes. Then on that Saturday night, after midnight, I got a text.

> You're going to want to be at church tomorrow. At the 9:00 a.m. service.

That's all it said, but I knew.

Something had been wrong at church for a while. For months, really. It had felt off, sort of like when a mystery food in the fridge has turned just a bit sour. That face you make when you open it and say, "Wait, what's going on in here?" is the same face I found myself making on a lot of Sunday mornings. Friends had slowly begun leaving our church, naming one reason or another.

I'd been at Cross Point for five years by this time. It was the longest and truest church home I had known in Nashville. Since I moved home from Scotland at the end of 2011, it had been my place. I served there, attended there, gave there. As with any place full of humans, I was hurt there and did some hurting myself. It let me down and it healed me. Our pastor was kind and loving, and I was really grateful for what God was doing at our church.

Until things started to change.

And that Sunday morning—the first time I ever saw church with my real LASIK eyes—the pastor told us he was leaving.

As part of a small group of friends who knew it was coming, we all sat together that day, right beside where the pastor would sit each Sunday. Connor was beside me, one of my best friends and Vandybros (shorthand for Vanderbilt University baseball players who are like little brothers to me). The pastor finally entered, halfway through the sermon being preached by our student pastor, Ketric. When the sermon was done, he slowly but confidently climbed the stairs to the stage.

I couldn't believe how clear his face looked up there. (LASIK is legit amazing.) He had been preaching to me for years and I'd never seen him more clearly. And he was leaving. With no warning, with no plan in place, leaving us immediately.

And my world spun.

I need a pastor. I loved my pastor. He and his family meant the world to me. I'd spent tons of time with them. They loved me really well. And the first time I was ever able to see him, his face wrinkled in ways I didn't know it could and tightened in ways I had never seen. And he said good-bye from stage.

For all the times we had hugged through the years, he didn't even look at me when he walked back down those stairs and out the door beside me, even though I was in his line of vision. For all the words and moments and memories we had shared, he left me with nothing but tears. It was an incredibly clear view of what it looks like when your pastor leaves.

———

My favorite roommate of all time is named Amanda. She and I grew up together. We were friends in middle school but really hit our stride in high school. Amanda's house was the place where I would accidentally spend the night for three nights in a row in the summer. Then after realizing a bathing suit and pajamas were not enough to sustain life, I'd go home for a few nights. We lived together one year when we were both at the University of Georgia, and then when she moved to Nashville in 2015, I begged her to move in with me and live in my guest room. She did. And my life improved drastically.

She showed up a few days before New Year's, the year it turned 2015. Lady Antebellum was hosting a dinner and playing the downtown stage in Nashville, so our group of ten girlfriends booked two hotel rooms and spent New Year's Eve in our own town. It was a great time for a new friend to move here—lots of fun activities, no one really at work, a memory-making couple of days.

Our living together life was a dream. I've had a lot of roommates over the years and was pretty worn out with it. But I knew Amanda would be different. We had so much history that when she moved to town, it was like my Nashville life completed in a lot of ways. Finally there was someone here who knew me and had memories with me before this was my town or my job or my life.

We lived together a year and a half before her company mentioned she might have to transfer back to Atlanta. My chest tightened the first time she told me, back in the spring. I did not *not* NOT want her to leave. But she did. October 1. Three weeks after LASIK, three weeks after my pastor left Cross Point.

My world spun again.

Okay, so when God had said *change,* I did not hear *loss.* And yet here I was, grieving the loss of two very important people in my life.

————

On October 18, my manager, Leigh, and I met for lunch at Peter's Sushi in Brentwood. We'd been trying to get together for weeks, but it just hadn't been working out.

I'll never forget the day, years before, when we were at an event together in Orlando. She worked for a record label, and my first book had just released. She had hired me to speak at an event, and we became fast friends. That day in Orlando, I was lamenting my need for more help with my career—some oversight, some direction, some strategic brains to come alongside me. Namely, a manager. I said, "I just wish it could be you, but if it can't, who do you suggest?"

She smiled. Said she had just left the music company, and she would be doing that exact kind of work under her own name. I became the first client for MaddJett, her management company.

That was in 2012.

Leigh was my brain and my sidekick. When things went awry with my literary agent, she stood beside me through the firing and separation from the old agent, and then the interviewing and hiring of the new agent. When multiple publishing deals were on the table to be considered, she helped me sort through that decision. When I needed to hire or fire someone, she talked me through it. When someone needed to talk to me about my physical and emotional health, she was the one.

And then, over a plate of sushi on October 18, she quit me. We both cried.

I got in my car very sad but mostly shocked. I didn't drive away at first. Just put my hands on the steering wheel and sat there. How in the world does another North-Star-type person leave my life like that? *That's three in five weeks, God. You're really doing a thing here, and it's killing me.*

———

And then a man I'd been dating called it quits.

And then I had to let an employee go.

And then my godfather died.

All before Thanksgiving.

———

I kept thanking God in my journal for the little heads-up He'd given me, for that repeated mention of change coming. For some reason, a few of the most important voices in my life cleared. Emptied.

My pastor.

My best friend.

My manager.

And this thing I'd been living and anticipating—the year of great love that was supposed to happen in that twelve-month window—now had less than a month. LESS THAN A MONTH.

———

Joe was my grandfather's first cousin. He and his wife, Earlene, were like another set of parents to my mom as she grew up. They had one son, who died tragically the same week I was born. To honor their loss and their relationship with my mom, my parents made them my godparents.

We saw them a few times a year for my whole life. They even let me ride with them across the country once, from Louisiana to Wyoming, when I was in the eighth grade, sealing a special place in my heart forever. (Because anyone brave enough to road-trip with a middle schooler deserves major props.) Joe was absolutely one of my favorite family members.

I sat in his room a few days before cancer took his life and told him all about what I had been teaching at conferences, what I was studying and writing. It was the week of Thanksgiving, and the day after I returned to Nashville, I was in the car again, headed back to Georgia for his funeral. During the service, the pastor read a quote my godfather had shared with him. He said it quickly, but it caught my attention immediately because he said it was a quote from a Scottish guy. I made a mental note to ask him for a copy of it before the day was out.

Southern funerals, you may know, are terribly sad occasions but with incredibly delicious luncheons afterward, as was the case for my godfather, Joe. The church fed us with their homemade fare: fried chicken and casseroles and potato salad and multiple types of cake. If any of it was bought in a store, they sure tricked my professional

Southern eye. I think it was all made in kitchens with love. Southern women cook like that.

Toward the end of the luncheon, I stopped the pastor and asked if I could get that quote from him. He kindly walked me across the church gym to where he had stashed his notes. The quote was from an old, old poem about the Scottish pirate Sir Andrew Barton.

During one of his pirate battles, Barton is believed to have said:

> I am hurt but I am not slain.
> I'll lay me down and bleed awhile,
> Then I'll rise and fight again.

And that was the phrase I repeated that day for two and a half hours driving back to Nashville.

Because it was how I felt. It wasn't like the past spring, when I'd felt like my life was numb with pain. This pain felt purposeful. It felt like God was letting me hurt and experience loss because this was making space for something. When two people leave your life in a short amount of time, you grieve and ask questions. When it's more than a handful of people in fewer than three months, you grieve and see God. You see the emptiness purposefully.

After returning home from the funeral, I went to dinner at Andrew and Alison's, the Osengas. Sadie was practicing cartwheels, Charlotte was plinking away on the piano like a five-year-old loves to do. Their oldest daughter, Ella, eleven years old, does incredibly beautiful hand lettering. So after dinner, I told her I'd heard these poetic lines that day and wondered if I could pay her to write them for me.

I asked how much it would cost, and at the same time I offered her twenty dollars, she said, "Two dollars." Her parents and I cracked up. We met in the middle and I paid her ten. And now on my refrigerator hangs a simple piece of paper with these three lines beautifully printed:

> I am hurt but I am not slain.
> I'll lay me down and bleed awhile,
> Then I'll rise and fight again.

I was feeling very alone at that time, pretty worried, and somewhat abandoned. I knew it was okay to lie down and cry about this, but also I had to get back up again. There was a month left to live in this year, and I was gripping as tightly as I could to what I knew about God and what it looked like to be fully persuaded.

This whole year had felt like one big game of Chutes and Ladders. A good roll would move me up a ladder, then a few bad rolls would send me down a chute. It hurt. Christmas was around the corner, and I was scared. Would the Groundhog Day, here-it-comes-again feel of the holiday season break my heart? Would the darkness of April happen again? Would I ever be protected from the wrestling that gave me such a limp?

———

I decided to mail Christmas cards. I absolutely love receiving them every year, and I hang them up on display in my house every holiday season. Almost all of the cards are from families, but I had seen some other single friends do it recently, namely my friend Kelli and her cat, Ruby. For years before she was married, Kelli unashamedly mailed friends and family a professional picture of her and Rubes, and we all loved it. I wanted to be part of one of my favorite holiday traditions, even though I don't have adorable children of my own or a handsome husband or a new Tudor home as backdrop for a festively posed picture on the front steps. (I don't even have a pet. They are so expensive!) I'd always put off the Christmas card idea. "Next year I'll be married SURELY, so I'll just do one then." And it just kept not being my reality each year when November rolled around.

I thought of it, or dare I say God whispered the idea to me, on a Friday in November while flying from Nashville to Kansas. As I eavesdropped on my neighbor in seat 10B, she flipped through her many printed pages of addresses, culling down her list of who would and would not be receiving 10B's family Christmas card this year (sorry, Ben Jackson + family).

The idea, as it percolated in my mind, brought tears to my eyes. Just before getting on this plane, when my assistant, Eliza, and I were standing in line for a drink at Starbucks, we had been talking about the holiday season that was fast approaching.

"I've got to do something different this year," I told her, "I'm not willing to rush through the holiday season in attempts to assuage the pain of another unmarried Christmas."

(I cannot with certainty tell you I used the word "assuage" here, but I wish I had, so please allow some author edits to conversations here and there, in hopes of someday sounding a bit more posh than I actually am.)

I know I'm not the only one for whom holidays have gotten progressively harder as the years pass. I think it's true for any of us who want something we don't have—be it a spouse or a child or a new place to live. Or it could be hard not because of what you don't have, but what you DID have last year. Whether you've lost someone in your family, gotten divorced, or had a massive shift in your circumstances, the holidays are time stamps, markers, and reminders of what you don't have, or what you used to have, or what you do have, like a bad medical diagnosis or a broken relationship.

And I just couldn't bear to think of riding on the carousel of holiday sadness again for two months. I had to break the cycle, do something different, allow myself to feel the sadness but have a plan in place that allowed for some celebration. I had to hop off that sad carnival ride and find a coaster that was way more fun.

And 10B showed me the fun and how to celebrate, even though she never knew. (Big ups to you, 10B. Thanks a mil.)

"So, I'm sending Christmas cards this year," I said to Eliza when we got off the plane. She was surprised but really liked the idea. I didn't know yet what it was going to look like. But I knew the idea of taking a picture of me standing alone by a decorated Christmas tree and mailing it on 5 x 7 postcards to a hundred of my closest friends felt really stupid. So I tried to think about what brought me the most joy. THAT is what I wanted on the card. What in my life represented the most joy of my year?

Ah, I knew it. The answer was easy. My friends' kids. The ones I live my life with. My mini-BFFs I call them—the offspring of my BFFs. I have a plethora of them, and they are absolute joy in my life. I love their little personalities and the way they laugh when we talk and the games they invite me to play. I've always been a big fan of kids. I had NO IDEA how that love would multiply when my friends began to multiply.

So, Annie, do you want to remember what you don't have this Christmas? Or do you instead want to celebrate some moments this year gave you?

You do?

Then make that Christmas card!

I got home at the end of that weekend trip and began to look through my phone for my favorite pictures over the last year. I was looking for the ones of me with my mini-BFFs to make into a collage of pictures for my first-ever Christmas card.

After getting permission from all the parents, I set to work, dropping the pictures into a layout created by one of those online photo websites. There was Ben and me in our Arsenal soccer jerseys on the top left. Jarrett and me eating sandwiches on the bottom right. The Osenga girls and me in our onesie pajamas, a yearly Christmas tradition, just above Molly's boys in their Halloween costumes. Parker and Sloane holding a copy of one of my books (don't you KNOW it was a shameless plug on my part), and Theo climbing up a ladder on the playground. The Hodges girls. Icees with the Whittakers. Getting nails painted with Carys and Mosie. Annabelle and Aury and Everly and Jude and Zanna. All collaged together like a yearbook from a school that most of them aren't old enough to attend.

Across the middle of the card, I put a text box and typed in:

IT'S BEEN A VERY MERRY YEAR!

I wrote a little note on the back about how much joy and love these little ones bring to my life. Finally I added a picture of my own face (because *just* enough single men were getting this card that it was worth dropping a professional headshot), and then signed each one. I mailed them out and it just felt good. It was so, so fun. I loved picking the fonts and the stamps and dropping them in the post office mailbox in groups of ten. The only person who expressed any disappointment to me was Jarrett, because when I'd called to ask if I could put our sandwich-eating picture on my Christmas card, he thought it was going to be the ONLY picture on the card. He was none pleased to find other children were also featured in my collage. (Fair. I've called him my best friend for the last eleven years, since the literal day he was born. I would have made the same assumption if I were him.)

The card was beautiful. I framed one for myself and put one in my Lovely Jar,[3] a token of the good things God did in my life that year. Getting to celebrate my people meant a lot to me, being a part of this holiday season in a way I'd always wanted. Somewhere in the back of my heart, deep down in my knower, I finally felt on equal playing ground with the people who seemed to have it all (or who have the "all" I want to have).

And for my heart, that was a great change.

11

This opening section is an actual excerpt from my journal during that season:

December 3

My counselor says I'm untethered, which may be why it seems like I'm falling. And it may be why I'm not feeling anything. Because I'm terrified.

I'm a fan of having an anchor person in my life. Maybe it's my enneagram number or my personality or my history of pain, but I often say I'm a balloon and I need a weight to hold me down.

It's not a bad thing. It's just the way I am. I'm not needy or massively codependent. I'm not irresponsible or flighty or annoying (I hope), though I am lightweight and fun and carefree. But that makes me deeply afraid of floating away. So I'm partial to having a person I can tie to, who can be my heavyweight, who won't let me float away. I don't mean I always need to have a man in my life, though I do like men a lot. It's more this: having a go-to person makes me really happy. I just want someone to hold on to me and someone who doesn't mind if I tie my string to them.

I just don't want to fall. I don't want to be out of everyone's grip.

———

Right before I moved to Nashville, I went to a concert in Atlanta where some Nashville artists were performing. My friend Heather and I bought tickets to see this group of singers and songwriters at an old church downtown. I didn't know these artists, but I knew they were Nashville and I knew I was moving there, so I decided to go to their show. It felt like a little baptism into the town—to sit in the crowd and listen to them sing to us, covering us with the sounds of the city where I would soon live.

Heather and I sat about ten pews back, off to the left side. I had no intention of speaking to any of the people performing (or attending, for that matter). I was just there to see Nashville in action, to prepare my heart for living amidst these humans.

Halfway through the show I realized both my hands were clenched tight. Subconsciously I was holding on for dear life to a dear life in Georgia that I didn't want to lose. I realized I was only weeks away from being, well, untethered. I realized in that moment, listening to Randall Goodgame sing, that I was about to pass through a doorway into their world, and the door back to my old life would lock behind me. Everything was about to change. And I would lose everyone. So my brain told my hands to HOLD ON. SQUEEZE. DON'T LET GO.

I slowly opened my hands, almost stretching them as if the muscles had constricted and I was just now being given permission to release them. I opened them palms up and pulled my fingers as far apart from each other as I could, creating starfish out of both of my hands. I laid them, open and palms up on my lap and tried to keep them that way. *You're going to be fine, Annie, I said to myself. Keep your hands open. Let go. You won't fall.*

It's been a decade since I opened my hands, and I don't regret it at all. And yet I've repeatedly felt like I was falling with nothing to grip.

———

I've been stretching my hands a lot this week too. The untethered feeling has returned, like that day in the pew ten years ago, and I keep grasping at people to be my life preserver, to preserve for me this life I don't want to lose.

I'm scared that without being tethered to someone, I'm going to become someone I don't like. It's sort of this mixed-up understanding of accountability—like, if I don't have a person who knows all the things about me and will hold me together, I'll fall apart. And right now, following the exodus in the fall, when things haven't gone the way I thought they would, I feel person-less. I feel a little as if God can't be gripped either.

After a hard evening of writing on Monday, I went to the grocery store and felt massively panicked that I was going to shop until I dropped (or gained ten pounds). I was forced to have some real conversations with myself:

> *DO NOT tether to food because you feel untethered from humans. DO NOT find in food a respite or a rest stop or a safe place to land. Food will not actually fill this empty you feel. It isn't meant for that.*

But I wanted to. I wanted to buy up the chip aisle and buy down the cookie aisle and not look back. I wanted carbs and chocolate and anything that could possibly make me feel better. But I've been on this journey long enough to know it never really works. (I also, to be fair, don't think "quiet times" work all that well either if you're artificially trying to anchor to them.) I grabbed one pack of ramen noodles (not the twelve pack, even though YOU KNOW I wanted it) and the smallest bag of marshmallows I could find. Gluten-free, dairy-free desserts are harder to acquire than you might think, so I'm thankful for a mallow every now and again.

As I got back in my car, I shot off a text to a single man in my life who shouldn't be held responsible for anything Annie-related (except making me laugh), but I begged him to be my anchor. I didn't use those exact words, but I did use some HELP ME language. And I knew, as soon as I hit send, the words I'd typed were my way of asking him if I could tie to his anchor for a bit. I was telling him I was about to float away if someone didn't grab me. And I was hoping he would grab me.

That's why I told my counselor about it. And that's when she told me I'm untethered. And that's when I realized I've been here before. Untethered. Only this time feels different. This time I almost feel like God has untethered me from other people on purpose, or has allowed me to untie myself from them, as part of something He's wanting to do in my heart right now.

What if I'm right? What if God's kindness is behind this untethering? What if His kindness actually looks like me feeling as though I'm just one breeze away from being blown off course? The marshmallows, the texts, the squeezed tight grips—they're all signs that the wind is blowing, and I'm living my life afraid that I could fly away from my faith.

> Prone to wander, Lord, I feel it.
> Prone to leave the God I love.

There must be something for me here. That's what I'm telling myself right now when I'm hurting, watching Netflix alone on a Friday night, trying to cry but the tears aren't coming. God doesn't intend to shift my life so that I fall apart. He intends to give me manna, to sustain me, to provide for me. But I don't feel provided for. I feel afraid.

And the layer under that fear is anger.

Here, I'm just going to say it. I'm so mad that after doing this faith thing for thirty years, and after getting dunked in the waters of Loch Ness with the promise that everything was going to be different—I'm mad that here I am, above water again, floating away. As if the years of my faith walk haven't made my muscles any stronger or my heart any braver.

But I know that's not true. I know this is the manna. I used to think the pain was a curse, but it isn't. It's a gift. It's His provision. Poet Mary Oliver said, "Someone I loved once gave me a box full of darkness. It took me years to understand that this, too, was a gift." I guess it doesn't make me feel less untethered to hear that. It just makes me not give up. It makes me believe in the power of persevering. It makes me believe there's *always* something on the other side of the pain and mystery.

———

I took a Saturday night to myself recently when my roommate was out of town and everything just felt good and quiet. This feeling of being so alone and sort of sad had me sitting on the couch, slumped to the side, resting on a pile of throw pillows. (I believe in the power of a couch covered in decorative pillows.) I flipped the television on, scanned through the channels, and stopped on *The Shack*, seeing it was available OnDemand. I had read the book a decade ago and remembered the story well, but had never seen the movie.

I wasn't trying to find God in my movie-watching that night. In fact, I was probably trying harder to check out than check in. But something inside me bumped when I saw that option, and I stuck with it for a little while.

One line I heard in particular made me pause and take note (and take notes, actually). The main character, Mack, goes back to the place where his child was murdered, and he asks God why he needed to come back here. Back came the answer: "Because here is where you got stuck."

In an instant I was blinked back to April, to the season of darkness, to the time in my life when I questioned God the most and wondered if He is really kind. And I realized how, in that season—yeah, I got stuck. Not majorly stuck, not desperately stuck. Just stuck. I got stuck back there where all my good works and all my striving weren't getting me what I wanted and couldn't get me out of my funk. My book didn't do what I wanted it to do, and my life didn't either. And my hand grabbed hold of that pain, that worry, that hurt. And I haven't let go of it yet. Untethered, and yet stuck.

Pretty nasty combination.

———

What stinks is that I didn't even feel tethered to a church at the time. In fact, I felt floaty. And scared. And I was angry about that too. It was the first time in my life I felt church-homeless.

Ever since our pastor left, it felt like I'd lost an umbrella. The thing about umbrellas is that you don't need them every moment. It doesn't rain every day. But when you do need an umbrella and you don't have one, you can get soaked pretty quick. And ever since the exodus—after all that untethering—I've felt soaked.

I drove around last week just thinking about all of this. It's not something I do often, but sometimes I just turn down roads I've never seen to get to places I've never been (or sometimes to places I've been a lot), and I think. I listened to a podcast about spiritual trauma, wondering if this whole church thing has been harder on my insides than I realized. And I think it has.

Because I couldn't cry. It's not that I didn't feel like crying; I just felt empty. Empty of tears, empty of emotion, empty of want, empty of any offering that someone could want from me.

When did the baskets of manna ever empty like this? Nothing to draw from, nothing to give, not sure what to do when the manna seems totally gone? To the point that it feels like the baskets which once held help and provision won't be filled again? Am I more and more of an Israelite instead of less?

When I thought about going to church (and this won't surprise you), I thought I wanted to go to a cathedral. In that moment when I had no pastor, no tethering, and no way to walk through those doors without being in pain, I just wanted to go somewhere old. Sturdy. Reliable. Ancient. I wanted to go somewhere that wouldn't hurt.

———

Yoga class was extra hard that day, the day he called to say he wasn't coming to visit me, the day my plans fell around me like sweat droplets from my elbows and shoulders and knees and eyes.

But no. That wasn't sweat from my eyes. It was tears. Tears of worry and sadness and wonder. Wonder how we got here? For me, I'm prone to wander and prone to wonder. Lord, I feel it.

I had never taken a yoga class from this teacher before. In all honesty, I had signed up thinking it was my favorite teacher, Emmy, but then some stranger chick came in and turned up the music and was asking me to do downward-facing dog before I even really knew her name.

The class was so hard. I hadn't been to yoga in a week or so because I'd been on the road traveling. So I knew it would be hard for my body before I even started. Getting back into the movements and the motions and the foreign shapes is not exactly like getting back on a bicycle. It's more like getting back in the dentist chair. You probably won't love it, but it's a good thing to do. So I knew that feeling was coming.

But the hardest part was what my heart was going through. People keep telling me we hold our emotions in our hips. I don't know if that's a woman thing or a yoga thing or what, but as class ended and we stretched more, as I bowed in a child's pose, my mind began to recap what was happening, and I couldn't control the tears.

The window shades slowly lowered as the climax of class passed and we headed into stretches. The room was dark, the fans were on, and I was wiping sweat from my head while wiping tears from my eyes as fast as I could.

And then I just quit.

I quit trying to wipe it all away, and I just laid there. I controlled my body by following the instructor's directions: turn this way, roll that way, put your arms here or there. But I didn't try to control my emotions. I let them go.

And the tears just poured. And I prayed. I talked to God because I didn't know what else to do in the silence of that room, lying alone on my mat. I told God how very disappointed I was feeling and how deeply sad this whole story had turned. I told Him I didn't know how we had gotten here, but that I was really, really sorry we were here. I told Him that things were supposed to be different than this, I thought, that the story made sense a few months ago. How did everything fall apart so slowly and so quickly at the same time? I wanted to ball up and pull the covers up over my head, but I wasn't at home. No covers to be had. So I just let the tears roll.

Class ended and I wiped my eyes and walked out rather quickly. Then just as I reached my car, the thought came to me, as if from God . . .

What if the pain is My provision?

What?
Wait.
No thanks.
Wait.
What if this pain is actually God's provision for me? How is THAT possible? How is that a thing? Oh yeah. The limp. The empty. His provision can be pain.

My friend Jamie texted me in the summer. She had no idea I was about to start the weeklong fast.

> Girl . . . heard that Hillsong song again,
> and the Holy Spirit just about stopped me
> in my tracks as I was getting ready this

a.m. That lyric about "freedom untainted"
and "no moment is wasted" is for you.
I had this thought of you jumping and
spinning around completely untethered
to a cord that was right beside you. It was
almost like a bungee cord. You had been
tethered to something by the cord and you
had been able to run from it but could only
get so far before it would yank you back.
I don't know what the cord was attached
to, but God was showing that you are
completely free now and that you can run
as far as you want without fear of being
constrained.

When being untethered is the gift. When the limp
is the blessing. When the most beautiful thing is not the
empty places being filled, but the empty places being seen.

12

It was just a few weeks before Christmas. Our church had been without a pastor for about ten weeks, and in those ten weeks I think we'd had, seriously, ten different guest pastors. Actually this transition period had been a beautiful picture of the church caring for each other but also an exhausting experience for everyone. Not only were we trying to heal as a people, we were meeting someone new almost every week on the stage. It was powerful and hard and good and sad.

One of our campus pastors, Chris Nichols, was speaking on this early Sunday in December, the second week of a series. He started by talking about the three wise men and the epiphany—the name for the traditional day on the church calendar when the wise men made it to Bethlehem. He retold the familiar story—baby Jesus, born in a manger, the star appearing in the sky, and the three wise men from the East following it to find the Messiah, then giving him gifts of gold, frankincense, and myrrh. (Sing with me: "We three kings of Orient are . . .") Then on the large touch screen behind him, Chris pointed to one word:

JERUSALEM

"When the three kings followed the star God had sent them, look where they ended up," he said. "In the wrong city. Well, at least, they ended up in a different city than where the Messiah was. They were in Jerusalem, not Bethlehem. And then the star disappeared."

My jaw almost hit the floor. How many times had I read this story and never put that together. They followed the star. They went EXACTLY where they thought it was leading them. And yet? They ended up in the wrong city.

Tiny detail when you read it on a page, but massive—absolutely massive—when you think about its implications for our lives. As Chris likes to say, "The cities were only six miles apart, but that's a real problem when the only information you have is that the baby is six miles from where you are right now, with no other directions."

So there they were. Stuck in Jerusalem. Going around and asking where the baby had been born, the one they knew was to be the King of the Jews.

How many times have you been absolutely sure you've followed God and heard His voice, and yet—here you are!—in the absolutely wrong place at the wrong time, and nothing makes sense at all.

That was me.

The whole sermon blew my mind—how sometimes when you're following God, even doing exactly what you're supposed to be doing can still land you in the wrong spot. Or at least not get you where you wanted to go. And yet sometimes, those are some of the best stories He tells.

Heartbreaking. Hopeful. True for me.

———

It was December 9.

Twenty-two days left in the year.

No man on the radar in my life at all. The ones who'd breezed in throughout the year had all left, and here I was, living as single as possible, with so very little time left.

I told God that morning, as I sat and prayed in my swirly chair, He was about to have a PR problem on His hands.

Only a handful of people knew what my year had been like, but enough of them were praying along with me that this wasn't just an Annie-and-God problem. This was going to be a crowd-and-God problem. How was He planning to explain to all the people in this story that we weren't in Bethlehem? How was He planning to rescue this story?

We had followed the star. I knew we had. In the deepest place in my soul, I knew I'd done exactly what God had asked me to do, and I was deeply expectant He would do the same. Surely He wouldn't let this story of faith and believing, this story of His voice and His kindness, end in a flop. I couldn't believe He would do that to me or my people.

Actually, the truth was I didn't think He would do that to me with such a large audience watching. It wasn't *me* I thought He would treat differently; it wasn't *me* I thought He would be faithful to. Honestly, I *did* believe He would do that to me. I'd felt it before—believing Him as best I knew how and still not ending up in Bethlehem. In fact, in some other stories that exist in my history, I never even got to leave Jerusalem. Disappointment seems to be too near of a companion for me, too easy an excuse, and too common a feeling.

But this time felt different because so many people were involved. It was all the people watching. What about them? Which is why I brought up His PR problem.

Then in the quiet of my soul, He seemed to say . . .

The year isn't over yet.

"That's awful," I responded. "Don't do that to me. Don't act like You're going to show up for me at the last second and then not do it. This is not fun anymore. You're hurting me."

Yes, I said all those things.

And then I chose to believe Him.

I thought about Lamentations 3.

I'll never forget the trouble, the utter lost-
ness, the taste of ashes, the poison I've
swallowed. I remember it all—oh, how well
I remember—the feeling of hitting the bottom. But there's one other thing I remember, and remembering, I keep a grip on
hope: GOD's loyal love couldn't have run
out, His merciful love couldn't have dried
up. They're created new every morning.
How great your faithfulness! I'm sticking
with GOD (I say it over and over). He's all
I've got left. (vv. 19–24 MSG)

Yeah. He was definitely all I had left. And I wasn't
even sure I could believe Him. I *wanted* to believe. I had
grabbed so hard to the words and really tried to live
fully persuaded that I was sure it would result in a trip to
Bethlehem. But here I was. In Jerusalem. Confused, sad,
frustrated. Probably a lot of the things the three wise men
felt too.

I called Lauren, the same Lauren who a year before
had told me this was the year for love. I told her all of
it: where I was, what I felt, how I was going to dive in
headfirst believing for twenty-two more days and come up
stronger for it.

"So crazy," she said, "one morning last week you came
to mind with your word for the year. I thought, *Did we*

misunderstand it? I will stake myself beside you in what you heard again. Trusting He is at work even now in your heart. Being open to receiving love. It starts first with Him, doesn't it?"

It starts first with Him. And here I was, barely hanging on to any hope. Just praying that He would come through. Hoping He loved me enough, *liked* me enough even, to be the kind of God who was kind to me.

———

That summer when the "bride" year had ended, I asked God for another word. I had so many questions around what that "bride thing" had even meant anyway, but I knew the calendar. My birthday was here, and it was time to ask for a new word.

This tradition had started the year I turned twenty-one. My twenty-first birthday was special. I was in Waycross, Georgia, at one of my best friend's homes, and he and his girlfriend (who was my roommate and bestie) went to a wedding during the day on that Saturday to which I was not invited. It was hot—July 7 is always boiling hot in the South—and so mid-morning I grabbed a plastic chair and dropped it into the shallow end of the family's swimming pool, then I followed it into the cool water. I pulled the chair over to the side, where my Bible and journal were laid down. I sat in the chair, perfect height for reading and for soaking, and opened the Bible on the hot cement. I asked God to meet me there. And He did. He's done it every year since.

My birthday that year, the love year, I was a little scared. So I sat in the swirly chair in my living room and asked for a word.

TRUST

I rolled my eyes, if I'm being honest. What a churchy Christian word. I wanted something outside the box, like MOUNTAIN or TIRE SWING, but here we were talking about TRUST. Then again, I guess if everything is about to change, you'd better trust the One who's changing it. You'd better hold on to any glimmer of "someone's got this" if you aren't the one who's got it. If it feels like you've ended up in the wrong city, you'd better trust someone knows what city you're in.

———

So Jerusalem didn't hold what the star promised. But, lucky for them, Jerusalem—still a great city—is a great place to end up, even if you're a trio of ancient Eastern astrologers who didn't find everything you'd felt led to be looking for.

I have a favorite corner in Jerusalem, and my mind goes there when I think of God's kindness and when I think of that city. The couple of times I've been there, we've stayed at Eyal Hotel. It's on an old city street made of cobblestone, but the hotel itself is very modern. It's truly the perfect combination of old and new, a beautiful representation of Jerusalem, both ancient and modern.

When you turn left out of the hotel and walk to the end of the street, you reach a dead end. Hanging above you, strung across the narrow, cobbled road, are umbrellas of many different colors. And so bright. Crazy bright. Green and yellow and pink and red and teal. Hundreds of them covering the air above our heads as we walk down the street. It's a little corner of the universe that brings me so much joy, so much beauty. Something about the colors and the shade and the brightness and the coolness. Walking down the street at night, the umbrellas shine, not from being lit but simply on their own. They just sort of glimmer. And when our crew would head back there after dinner, on a warm August night, we would lazily walk, no one in a rush, just meander down the street, letting each open parasol mean something for a moment.

They felt like kindness.

If that's what staying in Jerusalem meant, I could do that.

But in my heart, I realize seeing beauty in the wrong place doesn't make it the right place. But, gosh, don't I wish it did. Don't I wish I didn't long for the promise fulfilled in Bethlehem. But I do. So as much as I want to act like Jerusalem is enough to keep me from feeling disappointed, I will be. I know I will.

And I will wonder how to call God kind after a year like this.

13

I was driving from my cousin's wedding in Hershey, Pennsylvania, to the airport in Philadelphia. It was ten in the morning. I had an early afternoon flight to New York City and an overnight flight to Edinburgh to celebrate New Year's with my friends.

I felt complicated emotions. December 30. The year was ending. In fact, here was the end, staring right at me. And all the things I'd believed, all the words I'd thought were meant for this exact year, all the days I had pressed through the unbelief, all the times I'd chosen to be fully persuaded even when the story wasn't working out—they all blinked before my eyes. They all rubbed my heart raw. They all made me very sad.

Because it was over. I was hours away from flying to Scotland. All opportunity for God to do what I was fully persuaded He would do had left. And I wondered if He was kind.

———

I got an email this week, after asking listeners to my podcast if God was always kind. The subject line said, "God is not . . ." and then as I opened it, the first two words said, "Always kind."

God is not . . . always kind.

The writer of the email went on to explain why her life made it very clear that we are not dealing with a kind God.

Then on Instagram, just minutes after reading that email, I see my friend Courtney quoting Isaiah 54:8 about God's EVERLASTING kindness. Not even casual kindness, or often-displayed kindness, but everlasting kindness. The emailer doesn't believe that.

And on December 30, I wasn't sure I believed it either.

———

I rented a tiny little car to take me the couple of hours to the airport. I connected my phone with the Bluetooth and started listening to the podcast of a sermon from a church I love. I honestly don't remember much of the sermon, but I do remember the pastor asking a question as I traveled the lonely highway through the country parts of Pennsylvania.

"What do you believe about God?"

And immediately, before I even had time to ask God, a paragraph dropped into my mind. Before I even had time to think, it was there in full.

I think God strings me along. He tells me what I want to hear so I won't quit playing for His team. He doesn't actually intend to do the things He says, but He says them to me because it's what I want to hear.

He strings me along.

I couldn't get that phrase to stop repeating in my mind. And it broke my heart a little bit every time it did, because I knew if I was being honest, I deeply believed it was true. It felt very, very true. This paragraph had been bubbling up in my heart for a long time—waiting, I guess, for the right person to ask me the right question—or maybe waiting for me to have the courage to say what I was really feeling.

I tell people a lot, "God can handle your doubts and fears. He can handle your true feelings. Don't hold back." And I think I've always believed that. I've never questioned whether God could handle my doubts; I think I worried that *I* couldn't handle them. Like, if I actually said this stuff out loud—that God was just stringing me along in this life and in this story—my faith wouldn't survive it or recover from it. So I didn't say it.

But there, in the car, I knew the whole paragraph existed in the deepest part of me, even while I knew it wasn't true. I knew it wasn't the character of the God I'd grown to know and love over the last thirty years of my life. The God I met in the sanctuary of my church as a five-year-old, and the God I knew in the waters of Loch Ness, was not a God who lied to His kids to get what He wanted. He wouldn't lie to me, I knew it. So why was this paragraph so deeply embedded in my heart?

———

A few weeks ago a lightbulb in my room exploded. I mean, literally EXPLODED. Pieces of glass shot to every corner. It was in my shoes, all over my carpet, under the hair dryer, in my laundry basket, scattered across my bedspread. It shocked me, and I knew it was going to be a major pain to clean up. How would I ever find all the pieces? Ugh. But I grabbed the vacuum and broom and got to work. About an hour later, I'd picked up all the glass I could see.

But wouldn't you know it, early the next morning, as soon as I got out of bed, I stepped right on a small sliver of lightbulb glass. It slid into my heel pretty deep. I hobbled into the bathroom and grabbed tweezers to start rooting it out. So gross. So painful. And honestly? I probably could've walked on it and not died, but why let it stay embedded when I could get it out and start to heal? So I sat down in the chair in my room, took a deep breath, and went for it. Wasn't fun, but I got the glass out.

The same "get the glass out" principle applied to that slice of thinking that appeared with me in the car in Pennsylvania. This was something we needed to deal with. I knew it. And to be honest, I was grateful. I could've left that "God strings me along" paragraph in my heart, and I could have lived with it. It wouldn't have killed me. But God knew we needed to root it out so I could start to heal.

I paused the podcast and just drove for a bit. I sat there with the lie I'd believed. I heard it over and over again in my mind. I thought about what I learned at the singles workshop—the one from back in chapter 3—how when you believe a lie, you pray for it to be removed, and then you ask God what truth should be there.

I started the podcast back up, and the pastor said, "Ask God what is actually true about Him."

So I did. There in the rental car on December 30. No emotion, no tears. I just wanted to know what was true and what wasn't. I needed my mind to be set right and for the truth to determine where we were supposed to go next.

"Okay, God, tell me the truth here."

And in that still, small voice, that quiet place where God and I meet alone, I knew it. "God is kind to me."

God is kind to me.

That is absolutely what is true.

Even though I was driving out of Pennsylvania and was running out of calendar days—even though I was leaving behind this year where so many road signs had pointed toward a different ending than this one, I knew what was true. God is kind to me.

It didn't make me *feel* different. You know that, right? It wasn't that I suddenly was driving through rainbows, tapping my non-accelerator foot, glancing into the rearview at teeth that sparkled every time I smiled. Not at all. The drive to the airport was me repeating over and over what was true, implanting it in my heart, saying it, choosing it, long before it felt true.

———

I did the quick flight from Philadelphia to JFK, leaving me a couple of hours to wait around before my connecting flight to Scotland. I'd decided I wanted to spend New Year's Eve and the first few days of the year with my friends in Edinburgh. New Year's Eve celebrations in Nashville had started to feel a bit too predictable to me. A handful of single women wearing sparkly dresses, paying way too much to attend parties that got weird minutes after the clock struck midnight. Just didn't seem fun to me. I wanted out. I'd done it for approximately the last eight years with few exceptions (thank you, Melissa and Jesse, for the most fun NYE wedding ever!), but in general, the same thing every year. And every year I was reminded again that, yes, I was single, and so were all the girls with me, and this was not how I saw the next year going.

So I wanted to go home. To go to Edinburgh.

I'd purchased my flight in August, still assuming that God would do something in my love life before the end of the year. I didn't see how Scotland fit into the picture; in fact, I didn't think it did. I just thought I was headed over for New Year's to avoid the repetition of what I'd seen the years before.

I was sure (so very, very sure) that in this story line of my life, I had followed God like I was supposed to follow Him that year. I'd believed Him with my whole heart, trusted Him like my word for the year had told me, and lived life the best I knew how for a woman fully persuaded that God was going to do what He said He would do. And yet here we were. Not at all in the place we thought we would be.

Not. At. All.

The last day of the year. No promise fulfilled. No word come to pass. No indication that the star had led me anywhere near Bethlehem.

The only thing I knew that really felt good right then was the travel outfit I was wearing. My favorite: black leggings; brown boots; my maroon long-sleeve shirt; and a long, thick, black-and-white woven cardigan. It almost read like a blanket, and for that I was grateful, since my goal was to sleep over the ocean. I would casually wrap myself in my own clothing, cocoon away, and snooze. Till then, I'd picked my seat in the Delta Sky Lounge, grabbed a few snacks, and pulled out my journal.

December 30. On the way to Scotland!

I wrote pages about what had happened in the car ride. I wrote pages about what I knew to be true even when it didn't feel that way. I wrote pages about what it meant that the year was ending, the words had not happened, but God was (and is) (and will continue to be) kind to me.

I wrote it all down.

I'm looking at it now, at those things, in that journal. I can still picture exactly where I was sitting when I was writing it. In fact, I went back there, ten days later, returning from Scotland, in the same outfit, the same chair, to journal about a trip that had changed my life. A God that had shown Himself to be kinder than I knew. A God who always keeps His word.

14

I had a window seat on my flight to Edinburgh. I am such a window seat person. I want to watch the world outside for as much of every flight as I can. It still just amazes me what we're able to see that generations before us never saw. So I stare, thinking of how different the world must have looked to my great-grandparents who never flew over the Rocky Mountains, or watched the acres of farmland lay together like a patchwork quilt, or saw the shore of the United States recede from view.

There was an empty seat next to me because the Lord is gracious and compassionate, and across the aisle was a woman who was Scottish but lived in America. A folk musician, she was going home to play a concert of some sort and to see her family and friends. We talked a bit, but then I willed myself (with the help of medicine) to sleep.

We had left New York City around 10:00 p.m. and would be landing around 9:00 a.m. Edinburgh time. That sounds really perfect if you look only at the numbers and don't factor in time zones. If you DO factor in time zones, I was landing right in Edinburgh about three in the morning, according to my body.

Didn't matter to me, though. I was absolutely thrilled
to be heading back. That plane could not fly fast enough.
Soon I'd be seeing friends I hadn't seen in years. Soon I'd
be walking the streets of a town that meant so much to me.
Soon I'd be relaxing, knowing my phone wouldn't be able
to get much service, thus shielding me out of range from
the outside world whenever I wasn't on Wi-Fi. It all made
me very, very happy.

Harry and Esther picked me up from the airport
in Harry's truck. I knew the plan from there. We'd be
heading up to Boreland Farm on Loch Tay to celebrate
Hogmanay (the Scottish word for December 31), where
we'd stay for a few days before heading on to Edinburgh.
A bunch of our friends, about fifteen or so, would all be up
at the farm as well—other couples and some singles—most
of whom I knew well or in part, a few I didn't know at all.
We pointed north, grabbed a few more friends for the trek,
and shot off.

I was tired but not exhausted. My excitement for being
"home," along with my knowledge of the time zone differ-
ence, along with only getting a few hours of sleep, made
me feel like a crazy person—like a youth pastor after a lock-
in. What time was it? And was I allowed to be asleep right
now? And was there a way I could defeat jet lag today?
(Why do I ALWAYS think I'll be more powerful than jet
lag? I never am. Never ever.) I felt grungy, the way you

do when you've traveled all night and only washed your face upon landing, not having changed your clothes yet.

When we arrived, Harry grabbed my suitcase and we headed inside. Most of the crew at the farm had arrived that morning or the night before, so by the time we got there, the place was already bustling with activity. People were milling about the barn. Some were washing dishes. Soup was heating on the Aga.

Oh, do you not know what an Aga is? My word, it's one of my favorite things. An Aga is a massive cast-iron stove that NEVER TURNS OFF. It can be heated by either a gas or electrical source, but after being powered up for the first time, it doesn't take much. The Aga stays warm in your house year-round. There are different compartments in it, like ovens, that range in temperature. So once you've figured out the temperatures of its different areas, you learn to cook from anywhere on it or inside it. It's amazing. Donna had put apple cider on one of the eyes, and I smelled it simmering as soon as I walked in.

Scottish people don't often wear shoes inside of their homes, so the entryway of the farmhouse was covered in shoes. Tennis shoes. Wellies. Golf shoes. Boots. All a little muddy (because it always rains in Scotland) and all strewn about. I unzipped my boots as people began to appear in the doorways to welcome me.

I could have cried right there. What a relief to be home.

I met a couple I didn't know. Hugged my friend Kenny. And then a man who was lacing up his tennis shoes in the doorway, preparing to leave, reached out his hand, even though he was still bent at the waist, working at his shoestrings. "Hi, Annie. I'm Andy," he said.

I sort of recognized him from when I'd lived in Edinburgh several years earlier but couldn't quite place him. Then the memory came back to me in a flash. It was in a doorway just like this one, at Leisa's flat, when he had helped Donna move in. I was meeting Leisa for dinner, and as I passed this guy in the doorway, he had set down some boxes and introduced himself. We met, said hello, and then Leisa and I left. I remember thinking, *That bald guy named Andy was really cute.* But that was approximately the last time I thought of him, until here, standing in the hallway of the Loch Tay farm.

"Oh! Yeah," I exclaimed, "I know who you are," reminding him of when we met and how I knew his family. He just smiled as he finished putting on his shoes and said, "Yeah, yeah, I remember that." Then he headed outside.

I found the rest of my friends as I wove through the rooms of the farmhouse, attacking them with full-size bear hugs. And, of course, with many words. (I am, without question, the loudest person any Scottish person knows. Just ask.) Harry set my suitcase down in the room where I would be sleeping—a bunk room with four beds, one for each single woman present for the weekend. Settled, I headed back downstairs to eat lunch with everyone. Yes, it was almost time for the midday meal. Or, to my body, breakfast.

James, as usual, had made some sort of hearty meat and vegetable soup. He's the chef in our group, and I am not complaining about it one bit. The soup was amazing— though admittedly I was not a hard audience to please, because the fatigue and the hunger and the pure joy of being in Scotland combined to make his soup taste like the finest bite of my life.

After we'd cleaned up from lunch, people kind of headed in their own directions, though a few were already starting to work on dinner. I saw on the Aga some of the plans for the night's Hogmanay meal. Prime rib. Potatoes. Turnip greens. Oh, I was a happy little American.

I decided this was my chance for a shower. (Fifteen people and three bathrooms makes for complicated sched-uling.) And a nap. I really wanted to stay up to celebrate ringing in the New Year, and I knew it would only be possible if I slept for a bit. After a cold shower (I couldn't figure out how to make the water hot and was too tired to ask anyone to help me), I think I slept for about four hours.

I woke up to the smell of meat in the Aga. It was almost 5:00 p.m. I love lots of things about the Scottish people, but their appreciation for naps and sleeping late (a "lie in" as they call it) is high on the list. I had thrown on pajamas to sleep and hadn't bothered to dry my hair. So when I woke up, it was going in about fifty-two directions. Still, I barely did much to improve my appearance—a bit of powder, mascara, and a touch of blush so I didn't look like I had slept all afternoon (even though, clearly, I had).

I thought to myself how grateful I was to be putting on a massive oversized sweater and jeans instead of a sparkly dress. (Which. You know I LOVE sparkles. But not this year.) I loved the idea that it was New Year's Eve and I wasn't all done up. I even put on my thick, warm socks. This was going to be a comfy, casual turning of the year.

———

Everyone had mingled together in the kitchen with the Aga. It felt so warm. Not only was the room warm because of the massive stove, *we* were warm. *Home* was warm. I could sit quietly and listen to their beautiful accents and hilarious stories and just relax into it.

The whole lot of us ate and laughed and talked for a good long while. I didn't even know what time it was at any point. But I also didn't care. I knew we wouldn't miss midnight. Someone who was more in charge than I would make sure of that.

As midnight approached, we headed out to the barn. I shoved my phone into the pocket of my black peacoat, bundled up with a scarf and gloves, and slid on my navy-blue wellies that I'd purchased in New York City in a tiny store in the West Village. They were wearing down and weren't terribly comfortable anymore, but I brought them along anyway.

About forty other people were staying on the farm property in other cabins, and all had gathered in the barn. It was everything you're probably picturing—a raised roof, no walls, a dirt floor, a fire pit right in the middle with five or six picnic tables in a semicircle around it. Strung lights hung from the eaves, creating a border of the whole building. Drawing closer, I almost instinctively hung back for a minute before walking in, just to look at it. And to breathe the cold Loch Tay air, blowing up the hill from the lakeshore. And to watch my friends mingling with the others under the yellow hue of almost midnight around a fire.

James and Harry had purchased a proper amount of fireworks to shoot off just as the clock struck twelve. I was standing near Harriet, a young woman from the town nearby who'd become friends with my friends. A man I didn't know was wearing a kilt and carrying a bullhorn, which he blared as a warning to announce we were one minute from midnight.

And I realized something.

"Harriet," I said, a little panicked, "what happens at midnight here? Oh my gosh, I'm suddenly realizing . . . I mean, I know what to do in America, but I've never been here for Hogmanay, and I don't know what to do. What do I do?"

I was a little panicked.

She looked me dead in the eyes and said, "Oh," in her cute Scottish accent, "everyone *kisses*. Like, on the mouth. All the men will kiss you."

"WHAT!?!"

I was shocked.

"I AM NOT PREPARED FOR THIS, HARRIET."

I looked around the open-air barn, realizing that the few men I knew would NEVER (would they?) . . . and the ones I didn't know (would they?) . . . Aaaaaa! This all felt really intrusive and WEIRD, and I certainly had not gotten enough sleep in the last thirty-six hours to handle the situation well.

"Oh, Harriet," I said with a red face and panic in my voice, as the kilted bullhorn man started to count down from ten. "Oh my gosh, what is about to happen to me?!?"

As I tried to maneuver to where Harriet was stand-ing—between me and every man in the barn—she doubled over laughing. "I'm kidding!" she yelled, just as everyone was screaming in unison, "3, 2, 1 . . ."

HAPPY NEW YEAR!

I had been facing toward the fire pit in the middle of the barn, but as the fireworks made their first pop in the sky and people hugged (yes, some kissed) all around the barn, I turned outward toward Loch Tay. I pulled my phone out of my pocket and took a selfie to send to my nine girlfriends back home—me smiling in the front, clean face, clean hair, scarf tied tightly around my neck, Harry and Andy talking in the background with their backs to me.

"Look!" I said in the text message to the girls, "It's a new year here! Happy New Year!" Then I took a picture of the fireworks.

And for just one blink of one second, I thought about God, and about the year ending. And I said, sort of quietly, maybe not even audibly, I don't even remember. I just lifted my eyes a little higher into the stars and half-thought, half-said:

I did it. I believed You.

Fireworks exploded in the Scottish sky, marking a new year just beginning.

———

A few of us stayed up talking all night long in front of a medium-sized but respectable fire in the sitting room of the farmhouse. Around 5:45 in the morning, one of the guys made a good realization that we, in fact, had stayed up all night, and it would be wise to head to our beds because everyone would be waking up soon. So we all said good night, and I went into my bedroom, where all the other girls were long asleep.

It had been one of the most fun nights of my life. Laughter. Pizza. Connection. Conversations. A warm fire. It was more than I knew to dream up.

Suddenly, almost as soon as I laid down, my phone blew up with friends from America, texting to wish me, "HAPPY NEW YEAR!"

Because it was 6:00 a.m. in Scotland.

But it was only midnight in Nashville.

Oh yeah! I hadn't thought about that. Everything that had happened since midnight had happened in the year that was just ending. All the fun and laughter and kindness and connection. *And love.*

Yeah.

Love.

I'd felt love that night from my Scottish people, love as I'd never quite experienced it before. And I hadn't even noticed that God had snuck it inside the year He had said "love" would happen. He'd done exactly what He said He would do, exactly when He said He would do it.

There in the dark of 6:00 a.m. on January 1, I knew God was faithful.

And I knew He was kind.

And I knew everything had changed.

I told Him all of that. That I believed Him, and I wouldn't stop believing Him. That what He had just pulled off in Scotland, and across time zones before that, and in the kindness talk we'd had in the car before I took off from America . . .

I'd assumed He was going to let me down, but He hadn't. He hadn't let me down.

15

Friday morning in Edinburgh, I got on a train to England. I was visiting two cities in two days before returning on Sunday to fly back to America on Monday.

I arrived in Durham, England, in the early afternoon of January 6, and Caroline and Nathan were waiting there for me at the train station. I was beyond excited to get to spend twenty-four hours with them on this holiday, dear friends from Nashville who now live in Durham. It was around lunch time, so we dropped my things off at their house and grabbed a late meal, immediately diving into all the talk from home and catching up on our lives.

Something's so special to me about friends who can be apart from each other for months or years at a time and still pick right back up where they left off. This family is like that for me. In just a few minutes, their kids and I were pals, and Nathan and Caroline and I were talking faster than we could listen.

Nathan knows how I love history, and all things British really, so we toured Durham Castle first thing. Their daughter, Clara Anne, was three, Ben was barely one, and those two jokers hung with us the entire time. Never once did they complain or pitch a fit. The castle people are smart. They're accustomed to tiny kids being forced to do tours such as this, so around every corner and in every room was a small stuffed lion that Clara had to find. I was impressed—not only that the docents had thought of this, but how fast Clara found each lion! She beat me almost every time. (Fine, *every* time.)

We finished the castle tour and walked down the sidewalk, maybe thirty yards or so, to the Durham Cathedral. It was only three in the afternoon by then, but in January in England, the sun had already started to let us know it was done for the day. The sky was turning deeper grays and purples as a crowd of us entered the building. Nathan began telling me the history of the place, pointing out details of the décor.

In one of the back rooms, a woman wearing a robe walked up to us. Her nametag read "Marion," and she jumped right into our conversation, offering us more information and really chatting it up with Nathan. Before we were done with the afternoon, Marion had taken us around the cathedral and even into a room that visitors don't usually see. She showed us the courtyard, used as the setting for Harry Potter's Hogwarts school, and brought us back inside.

Darkness had fallen. Nathan offered for Caroline and I to stay for Evensong, a nightly service they do at the cathedral. We said good-bye to him and the kids and took a seat in the choir loft. (Remember me saying a cathedral is laid out like a cross? Picture the four sections of a cross; we were sitting in the top.) I was super giddy. The chairs we sat in were those regal-looking wooden ones, with ornate designs to your left and right, even above your head, as if you've sat down in your own little wooden cave. Other people were also taking their seats for Evensong, but being a Friday night, the crowd was scarce. Maybe ten in attendance—five or six on the same side as Caroline and I; five or six in similar seats across the aisle. We were all facing each other. Marion then walked down the center, now, wearing commoners' clothes, her brown robe draped over her arm. She smiled at us and took a seat across the way.

The choir filed in, about forty of them, wearing their robes. They sat on both sides of the aisle as well, between us and the main part of the cathedral. The three priests followed after that, each in their ornate and beautiful robes. But the place they spoke from was off to the side from us, so we couldn't see them.

How different from my church, I thought. Our church has flashy lights and a band and lots of themed preaching series with fancy backdrops, so this wasn't my normal experience. This service was traditional and liturgical. Old Testament reading, organ, choir, New Testament reading, organ, choir. Really beautiful. I was trying to pay close attention to the Scriptures, trying to see if God was really going to show up in this place.

He shows up in cathedrals still, doesn't He?

———

Old cathedrals sometimes don't feel alive to me anymore, you know? I love walking through and touring them, trying my best to picture a time when it was just the local church. But they mostly feel like a museum to something that doesn't exist anymore. Maybe that's how I've felt about God at times too. More historic and memorable than alive.

That's the initial vibe I was getting that night at Durham Cathedral. But then something started to stir. I knew it. The Holy Spirit was telling me to lean in. To focus. To pay attention. To choose to connect.

After the Old Testament reading, a man I couldn't see from where I was sitting stood up to pray. "We're going to pray for three specific groups today." *Okay.* "The first group," he said, "are people who use words for their jobs."

My eyes bugged out.

I turned to Caroline and whispered, "Wait, what did he just say?" Her face told me she'd heard the same thing. The man continued.

"Whether it is in books or on stages, maybe even social media . . ." I don't know what he said to complete that sentence, because by then I was crying. So was Caroline. All of a sudden I knew God had brought me here on purpose. On this night.

I mean, in a service of no more than fifty people, how could this guy have known an author, speaker, and SOCIAL MEDIA LOVER was one of those people? And not a local. An American. And not a regular. A once-in-a-lifetime visitor.

It was too much for me. I leaned my head into my hands as the tears fell.

Then the man said he was going to pray.

I immediately started panicking. Do I close my eyes? Do I open my hands and receive what he's praying for me? Do I just listen and try to memorize it? Do I record it on my iPhone so I don't forget what he says? Do I grab my journal from my bag and try to write down every word?

All these questions ran through my mind in a split second.

The man sitting to the left of Caroline had a video camera going. I remembered we'd mentioned it when we sat down. So I decided if I wanted a copy, I'd be able to get one. From him maybe.

But I knew this was a holy moment—a moment meant for me, not to be missed. I needed to open my hands, open my heart, open my ears, and just let this man pray for me.

> O God, Your incarnate Son, Jesus Christ,
> is the eternal Word in whom may be read
> the good news at the heart of all that You
> are doing. Grant to all who speak or write
> what many may hear or read, that love of
> truth which leads to love of God, and that
> love of God which makes communication
> of thought a good and holy thing, through
> Jesus Christ our Lord. Amen.

Caroline had put her hand on my back and prayed along with me. And when the man we couldn't see said "amen," she and I looked at each other, tears streaming down our faces.

"Caroline . . ." I said, barely above a whisper.

"I know, I know . . ." was all she could say back to me.

He next prayed for "peacemakers," then for those who'd lost a loved one over the Christmas holidays. Typical categories, not like the first one—which was actually really good for Caroline and me, as we definitely needed to give our emotions some time to calm down.

The service ended and we both sat there, absolutely stunned. We could not believe such a clear moment had just happened. This whole trip to Scotland and England had been, for me, an over-expression of God's kindness. And tonight, the prayer at this Evensong service felt completely over the top. More than I could have asked or imagined.

———

I've always loved that verse. I think many of us do.

> Now to him who is able to do immeasurably more than all we ask or imagine, according to his power that is at work within us. (Eph. 3:20)

Earlier that week, once the year had officially started in Scotland AND in America, God had brought this verse to my mind over and over. For the first time I'd looked up The Message version.

> God can do anything, you know—far more than you could ever imagine or guess or request in your wildest dreams! He does it not by pushing us around but by working within us, his Spirit deeply and gently within us.

WHOA. I'd been scribbling those first few words into my journal almost daily since that night at Loch Tay: "God can do anything."

More than my wildest dreams.

———

Caroline and I sat there for just a few minutes more, long enough until Marion got up from her seat and walked straight across to us.

"How was the service?" she asked suspiciously. And rightly so! Here were these two American women, all weepy at the end of a typical service, one they conduct every single night in that cathedral. And probably without the emotional meltdown. She wasn't prying, it didn't feel like. It felt more like she was a mother hen checking on us after a storm.

I explained to her who I was and what I did for a job and asked if there was any way to get a recording of that prayer the man I couldn't see had prayed.

She smiled. "Would you just like to come meet the Archdeacon of Durham Cathedral?"

Why, yes. Yes, ma'am. Yes, that's exactly what I would like to do, please and thank you. Meanwhile my mind was screaming, WHAT IS GOING ON HERE? I was about to meet the man who holds a position in the Church of

England that's existed since approximately AD 1080. (Not the same dude, but same job. Just to make that clear.)

Caroline and I followed Marion to the three men standing in a row at the altar, each of them wearing a uniquely designed robe. The archdeacon's was a mix of golds and browns and whites and blues.

"Archdeacon Jagger, I'd like to introduce you to Annie," Marion said. He and I shook hands, then tears came to my eyes as I started to speak to him. I swallowed them back, quickly wiping away the ones already dripping down my cheeks.

"Hello," I said quietly. "My name is Annie, and you couldn't have known this, but I'm an author, and—"

Before I could finish, his eyes instantly widened. And with the seriousness that comes from seeing a long-lost friend, he gripped my hand tighter.

"It's you," he said.

I could hear Caroline crying.

"It's you," he said again.

I couldn't stop crying.

"I knew tonight was the night I was supposed to pray that. I've known it for weeks."

What kindness in his eyes. And to think that God had been talking to him about me.

"It's you," he'd said.

God's kindness. Everywhere.

His kindness was following me everywhere.

———

Bursting into their home, I yelled to Nathan, "YOU ARE NEVER GOING TO BELIEVE WHAT HAPPENED!"

"Well, I can't wait to hear," he said, "because today is Epiphany, so I've been here praying that God would give you an 'epiphany.'"

Caroline and I were both blown away. We could hardly form words. *Today is* . . .

EPIPHANY

Of course it is. Of course it is.

January 6–the day we remember those sojourners finally made their way to Jesus in Bethlehem. And while it may not have all made sense to them in the moment, Epiphany was the day their journey took on meaning.

It was all too much for me. Again.

A deep and profound empty space in me had been filled. Not by a man, not by The List, not by my own successes or thoughts or failures, but by an epiphany of God's kindness. By the reality of it.

He'd met me in a cathedral . . . so I'd always remember.

Epilogue

"And now, here's what I'm going to do: I'm going to start all over again. I'm taking her back out into the wilderness where we had our first date, and I'll court her. I'll give her bouquets of roses. I'll turn Heartbreak Valley into Acres of Hope. She'll respond like she did as a young girl, those days when she was fresh out of Egypt." (Hosea 2:14–15 MSG)

I'm back in Scotland, but it's October, and this is the first time since I moved away that I've been here twice in one calendar year. All those years ago, I'd sat in this same Starbucks in Holy Corner, just down the street from my flat on Mardale Crescent, and written *Let's All Be Brave*. Today is very different from those days. *I* am very different from those days. But this trip feels really important. (I'm not moving here this time, to be clear, but the coincidence of it is worth noting.)

I sat in this same coffee shop nine months ago to the day. Literally. To the day. The day before I took a train to Durham, England. The day before Epiphany. And I am here again. I choose not to ignore these things. I originally typed "you can't ignore these things," but you can. It's up to you. You are welcome to ignore the little moments that might mean something if you want to. I just don't want to.

Nine months. A baby. A birth. In fact, I'm back in Edinburgh because a baby *was* born to some dear friends, and I wanted to meet her.

That's what happens in nine months from conception. Something is born.

And I have to wonder . . . what has been born from this? From this season of my life? From the year of believing, but not really getting what I believed for? From the year where the limp became a blessing. From the year when my faith was tested, and God's faithfulness was tested, and I'm not sure we both came out looking all that great. (Though, to be fair, God pulled off a major to-do there at the end.)

So what has come of this?

A book? Yes. Technically. I started writing it here and I will work to finish it here. The first few words that I tried to stamp out here in January from the table in the corner by the window looking over to Holy Corner weren't any good, but I wrote them here. I don't believe God walks me through seasons just for the sake of a book, so that's not the main thing I think He wants me to notice.

A new relationship? Not the one I pictured I'd write about when I sat here on January 4, that's for sure.

But something has been born.

I felt it last night while Harry and Esther and Ciara and Harriet and I sat in the cheese shop in Morningside over a supper of sandwiches. I feel different. I feel stronger and surer. I feel like there's a secret in my soul that I don't have to tell but has totally changed the landscape of my heart.

I grieve a little too, sitting here today. I grieve over what wasn't born. I grieve over the hope that was conceived but miscarried. I grieve for the mirage of the Promised Land that was actually just another lap in the desert.

That's why I have to ask what was born. That's why I have to dig into the truth that, yes, something happened here and, yes, it mattered and, yes, there's something here for my hands to hold.

I need to take a deep breath and hold this tension, this place where things did work out and didn't work out at the exact same time. The tension when the limp is the blessing. Where, in some respects, I left a desert behind and in other ways, I'm still kicking sand.

And the more I wrestle down what the new thing is that I'm holding, the more I realize it's me. I'm different. I sit taller.

And all of that is well and good, but it's not the ending to the book I wanted to give you. This happened to me last time too. I couldn't finish the book. And recently as I sat in my counselor's office and talked about the fact I cannot finish the book because life doesn't look right and it doesn't end the way I wanted it to, she just looked at me, smiling, nodding, jotting down notes on her yellow piece of paper.

I moved on from that topic to another, to a new man. To explaining just how purely good he is. To talking about how deeply overwhelmed I am at the idea that he exists, that we existed together in the same world but just didn't know each other. Didn't see each other. Until now. But I don't know what happens next. There is mystery. There is a chance he's Bethlehem, and there is a chance he's Jerusalem. Maybe he's the blessing, or maybe he's the limp. Or maybe I will limp after this, and that will be a blessing.

But I do feel fear. And I'm afraid to hope.

I told her about my word for this year. You know it usually gets dropped in my heart on my birthday morning as I'm connected to God and celebrating, well, me. But this year, it came early. It was quite a . . . *surprise.*

After last year's fast, which started right before my birthday, I decided I wanted to make it a yearly tradition. Take a quiet week, focus and pray, get some direction and guidance for my next year on the planet. So I added the fast to my calendar for late June, but booked it pretty early in the spring so I'd remember not to fill that week with plans (or dinners!). And the week before, mid-June or so, I sat down to journal, and was just casually journaling about the fact that my new word would be born soon.

And then it was in my mind.

Surprises.

"Surprises?" I said. "That's a super weird one." And immediately I went into all the ways this word was going to disappoint me—probably a tragedy of some sort where I'll just have to say, "Well, God told me this year would be full of surprises, so . . ." Or where everything will fall apart professionally and I'll have to say, "Well, I was warned. SURPRISE! You have no career anymore!"

I told all that to Jennifer, the counselor, how the word for this year literally surprised me a month early. How I was sure it was going to lead to bad things. And she put her hand up like a stop sign.

"Stop. This is why you can't finish this book about God's kindness. Because you don't believe it. He told you SURPRISES? And you heard tragedy?"

She's right. I don't have a grasp on this like I want to. It's the limp making decisions for me, warning me I could get injured again, instead of reminding me I could get blessed again. My expectations mix with my fears, and my past failures mix with this life I can build in my mind's eye, and I'm just so scared to hope. I'm so terrified to picture joy and good things coming from that word when getting let down has become my normal. I jump in with both feet, expecting God to do what only God can do. And then it doesn't look right. It flops, as my brain thought it wouldn't. Or thought it would. And that's the hard part.

———

Jon and I sat across from each other at The Red Bicycle, and I couldn't control my tears. It all felt like too much, getting to this part of the book, this part of my life story, and it not looking right.

I don't know how to tell you this.

Books are supposed to end with bows tied tightly, with "All is well" typed solidly on the last page.

But all is not well.

I'm brokenhearted. The new man is not working, and I'm in more pain than I've experienced in a while. In fact, I said to Jon, "I've only felt this kind of pain and tension twice in my life, and both times I ran from it. Like, really ran from it. Like, got on a plane and flew away from it."

But it's the end of the story, so it should all be well.

But all is not well.

I'm still waiting for God to show up for me. I'm still wondering if He's going to spend my life breaking my heart. I'm still wrestling with Him because this doesn't all feel fair or right, and I'm ready for it to be fair and right and well. I'm tired of limping and I'm fatigued with the idea that this limp is with me forever, and I'm frustrated that I can't see it as a blessing.

I tried to wipe my tears, but it got pretty useless after a while. The slow roll of the stream down my face wasn't worth stopping. It felt exhausting. Everything does. Jon has been a dear friend for a long time, so he wasn't surprised or scared. In fact, he looked me squarely in the eyes and said, "You are not too much for me," which is maybe the most loving thing anyone has said to me in my life. Especially today, when I'm in a place of pain and tension that has no resolve, and I'm just rather sure that what is going on in me is too much because I am too much.

I've lived every story you've read and every page you've turned, and I don't think either of us thought I would be here, still wondering. It feels like too much.

I have to decide if I love God or if I feel chained to Him. I have to decide if He is kind, after all of this, or if He isn't.

But you know what? That's not actually the question. I don't wonder if His character is kind; I wonder if He will be kind to me in the way I want Him to be kind. I wonder if the Promised Land will actually hold promises that my heart has longed for or if it'll just be another place where I don't know how to live.

Jon watched me cry, and watched as I manage to simultaneously wipe my tears and eat breakfast tacos. He said he gets it, the fear of leaving you, my reader friend, without an ending that sets me up as strong and capable and full of belief.

Instead, I'm telling you what is sadly and disappointingly true (to me): in God's kindness, in His mercy, in His unfailing love toward me, I find I am incredibly weak and unresolved. I find I'm still wrestling even though I think my hip is way past broken. I will limp from here on out. And maybe one day, I'll call it all a blessing.

Because I'm pretty sure it already is. Because I will remember what we have been through, me and God. I will remember the limp and the blessing and the days and words and the years. I carry it all with me. Even in pain, even in worry, even today, wherever I am, I will not forget what He has done for me and been to me.

I will remember God.

Acknowledgments

I'm sighing again, whispering out thank yous to so many people who walked with me through this season and through this book. I won't name them all. You'll see them in the book and on my Instagram and hear of them on the podcast. But I am grateful deeper than I can breathe.

To the Downs Books Inc team, thank you for holding our work and our company with such determination and heart.

To everyone at LifeWay, thank you for holding this book with such tenderness and kindness and trust. (Particularly you, Lawrence.)

To my dear friends and family, thank you for holding me when I almost fell apart (whether you knew it or not).

To my miniBFFs, you don't even know how much hope and joy you bring into my life. But you will. I will keep telling you. A lot.

To you—the reader, the listener, the friend on the other side of the work I do, thank you for always showing up and being in this with me. It matters to me. Every time.

All thanks, really, to God, who invited me to this story that I would have never picked for myself. I had no idea how loved I was until You. Until now. Until this. I would do it all again for who I have found You to be.

Notes

1. https://www.forbes.com/sites/carriekerpen/2017/07/29/stop-comparing-your-behind-the-scenes-with-everyones-highlight-reel/#90609b03a073

2. John Ortberg, *I'd Like You More If You Were More Like Me* (Carol Stream, IL: Tyndale Momentum, 2017), 169.

3. In my book *Looking for Lovely*, I write about how I have a jar in my house where I keep little memories to help me remember the best moments of my life. You can read all about it in that book!

CHECK OUT THE NEW SEASON OF *THAT SOUNDS FUN* ON THE RELEVANT PODCAST NETWORK. IF IT SOUNDS FUN TO ANNIE, YOU'RE GOING TO HEAR ABOUT IT.

Also from Annie F. Downs

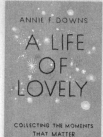

AVAILABLE JAN 2019   AVAILABLE JAN 2019